Safe Use of Machine Learning for Air Force Human Resource Management

Volume 4, Evaluation Framework and Use Cases

JOSHUA SNOKE, MATTHEW WALSH, JOSHUA WILLIAMS, DAVID SCHULKER

RAND PROJECT AIR FORCE

For more information on this publication, visit **www.rand.org/t/RRA1745-4**.

About RAND

RAND is a research organization that develops solutions to public policy challenges to help make communities throughout the world safer and more secure, healthier and more prosperous. RAND is nonprofit, nonpartisan, and committed to the public interest. To learn more about RAND, visit www.rand.org.

Research Integrity

Our mission to help improve policy and decisionmaking through research and analysis is enabled through our core values of quality and objectivity and our unwavering commitment to the highest level of integrity and ethical behavior. To help ensure our research and analysis are rigorous, objective, and nonpartisan, we subject our research publications to a robust and exacting quality-assurance process; avoid both the appearance and reality of financial and other conflicts of interest through staff training, project screening, and a policy of mandatory disclosure; and pursue transparency in our research engagements through our commitment to the open publication of our research findings and recommendations, disclosure of the source of funding of published research, and policies to ensure intellectual independence. For more information, visit www.rand.org/about/research-integrity.

RAND's publications do not necessarily reflect the opinions of its research clients and sponsors.

Published by the RAND Corporation, Santa Monica, Calif.
© 2024 RAND Corporation
RAND® is a registered trademark.

Library of Congress Cataloging-in-Publication Data is available for this publication.
ISBN: 978-1-9774-1289-8

About This Report

The Department of the Air Force (DAF) has begun to develop and field artificial intelligence and machine learning (ML) systems for myriad mission areas and support functions, including human resource management (HRM). ML systems have the potential to accelerate existing decision processes and to enhance decision quality by leveraging data. Further, by allowing the DAF to make decisions at greater speed and scale, ML systems may enable entirely new decision processes.

Notwithstanding this transformative potential, ML systems present a unique constellation of safety concerns in the HRM domain, compared with other information technologies. We identify three qualities of a system that, taken together, constitute our definition of *safety* in the DAF HRM context. To develop and field ML systems responsibly, the DAF must ensure that systems are (1) accurate; (2) fair; and (3) explainable. *Accuracy* means that the ML system correctly predicts the outcome of interest, *fairness* means that the system operates equitably for individuals from different demographic groups, and *explainability* means that a human can understand why the system arrived at the predictions or decisions that it did.

To provide assurances about the safety of ML systems for HRM, the DAF needs methods to measure accuracy, fairness, and explainability, along with implementation design patterns to engender these attributes. This report describes a framework to evaluate and augment the safety of ML systems for HRM. The framework is demonstrated using examples of ML systems designed to facilitate DAF promotion and developmental education board processes.

This research was commissioned by the Director of Plans and Integration, Deputy Chief of Staff for Manpower and Personnel, Headquarters U.S. Air Force (AF/A1X) and conducted within the Workforce, Development, and Health Program of RAND Project AIR FORCE as part of a fiscal year 2022 project, "Machine Learning Decision-Support Tools for Talent Management Processes."

This is one of five related reports originating from the project—the four companion studies are (1) *Leveraging Machine Learning to Improve Human Resource Management:* Vol. 1, *Key Findings and Recommendations for Policymakers* (Schulker, Walsh, et al., 2024); (2) *Machine Learning in Air Force Human Resource Management:* Vol. 2, *A Framework for Vetting Use Cases with Example Applications* (Walsh et al., 2024); (3) *The Personnel Records Scoring System:* Vol. 3, *A Methodology for Designing Tools to Support Air Force Human Resources Decisionmaking* (Schulker, Williams, et al., 2024); and (4) *Machine Learning–Enabled Recommendations for the Air Force Officer Assignment System:* Vol. 5 (Calkins et al., 2024) (see table). These closely related volumes share some material, including some definitions and descriptions.

Outline of Report Series

Volume Number	Report Title	Report Purpose
1	*Leveraging Machine Learning to Improve Human Resource Management: Volume 1, Key Findings and Recommendations for Policymakers* (Schulker, Walsh, et al., 2024)	Overview for senior leaders
2	*Machine Learning in Air Force Human Resource Management: Volume 2, A Framework for Vetting Use Cases with Example Applications* (Walsh et al., 2024)	Framework for how to prioritize ML projects
3	*The Personnel Records Scoring System: Volume 3, A Methodology for Designing Tools to Support Air Force Human Resources Decisionmaking* (Schulker, Williams, et al., 2024)	Technical report on scoring officer records
4	*Safe Use of Machine Learning for Air Force Human Resource Management: Volume 4, Evaluation Framework and Use Cases* (Snoke et al., 2024)	Case study approach to ensure safety of ML systems
5	*Machine Learning–Enabled Recommendations for the Air Force Officer Assignment System: Volume 5* (Calkins et al., 2024)	ML system to inform officer assignments

NOTE: Current report is highlighted.

RAND Project AIR FORCE

RAND Project AIR FORCE (PAF), a division of the RAND Corporation, is the Department of the Air Force's (DAF's) federally funded research and development center for studies and analyses, supporting both the United States Air Force and the United States Space Force. PAF provides the DAF with independent analyses of policy alternatives affecting the development, employment, combat readiness, and support of current and future air, space, and cyber forces. Research is conducted in four programs: Strategy and Doctrine; Force Modernization and Employment; Resource Management; and Workforce, Development, and Health. The research reported here was prepared under contract FA7014-22-D-0001.

Additional information about PAF is available on our website: www.rand.org/paf/

This report documents work originally shared with the DAF on September 13, 2022. The draft report, dated September 2022, was reviewed by formal peer reviewers and DAF subject-matter experts.

Acknowledgments

We thank Gregory Parsons (AF/A1X), Col Laura King (AF/A1H), and Doug Boerman (AF/A1X) for their support throughout the project. This research benefited greatly from their input and support. We are deeply appreciative of the assistance we received from many personnel, including Lt Col Monique Graham (2022 RAND Air Force Fellows Program). Finally, we thank the many RAND colleagues who helped with this work: principally, but not exclusively, Melissa Baumann, Benjamin Boudreaux, Benjamin Gibson, Lisa Harrington, Elicia

iv

John, Ignacio Lara, Nelson Lim, Miriam Matthews, Al Robbert, Sean Robson, and Peter Schirmer.

Summary

Issue

Private-sector companies are applying artificial intelligence (AI) and machine learning (ML) to diverse business functions, including human resource management (HRM), to great effect. The Department of the Air Force (DAF) is poised to adopt new analytic methods, including ML, to transform key aspects of HRM. Yet ML systems, as compared with other information technologies, present distinct safety concerns when applied to HRM because they do not use well-understood, preprogrammed rules set by human resources (HR) experts to achieve objectives. The DAF cannot confidently move forward with valuable AI and ML systems in the HRM domain without an analytic framework to evaluate and augment the safety of these systems.

Approach

To understand the attributes needed to apply ML to HRM in a responsible and ethical manner, we reviewed relevant bodies of literature, policy, and DAF documents. From the review, we developed an analytic framework centered on measuring and augmenting three attributes of ML systems: accuracy, fairness, and explainability. In this report, we define *safety* by these three qualities. We then applied a case study approach; we developed ML systems and exercised the framework using the examples of officer promotion and developmental education boards.

Key Findings

- For any given HRM process, AI systems can provide different types of decision support via many possible implementation designs. The choice of implementation design affects both the effectiveness of the system and its level of safety. Our framework helps HR managers choose the AI system design that best satisfies objectives while also meeting safety criteria.
- In many cases, but not always, the three safety principles of fairness, accuracy, and explainability might be in competition with one another. For example, limiting how model outputs are used may increases fairness, and limiting model complexity may increase explainability. However, placing such limits on how a model functions could reduce accuracy.
- With the case study of selection board processes, there are many different types of decision support that AI systems can provide. The possible options present different opportunities to reap business value, but they also have different risks.

- Multiple strategies are available to evaluate the performance of ML models, human raters, and joint human-machine teams.

Recommendations

- **Before implementing an ML system, the DAF should specify the HRM objectives motivating the application.** Projects should begin with desired objectives and measures of effectiveness, allowing the design process to produce a system that best achieves the objectives in a safe manner. Beginning a project with a preselected implementation design risks leaving value on the table or courting failure from a more ambitious design that cannot meet safety criteria.

- **The DAF should define acceptable limits for *accuracy, fairness*, and *explainability* and clarify the importance of each.** Broad AI adoption in the HRM domain cannot occur unless developers have clear guidelines on safety criteria that they must meet. The DAF can encourage broader development by publishing acceptable limits for safety criteria in accord with institutional values, giving developers confidence that designs meeting these criteria will be accepted.

- **The DAF should follow an implementation strategy that involves applying ML to limited cases before gradually expanding the scope and consequence of applications.** Though low-risk, low-impact applications might not achieve the maximum business value initially, they could provide an "on-ramp" for systems and allow members of the organization to become familiar with them and provide essential feedback. Thus, implementation strategies could begin with these cases and gradually expand the scope of the systems' use as they prove themselves trustworthy.

- **The DAF should use an iterative framework to select, design, and evaluate ML systems.** The framework embodies two principles that the DAF should adhere to when applying ML to HRM. First, set the final tests in advance (i.e., safety and effectiveness), and build the system to the tests. Second, incrementally refine the system as it is tested to balance the trade-off between safety and effectiveness. The DAF may need to reconsider objectives if the safety evaluations show they are not feasible.

- **The DAF should invest in means of generating automated summaries of narrative text contained in performance evaluations.** This implementation design offers a flexible way to meet numerous HRM objectives and can be used by itself or in conjunction with other implementation designs. With appropriate safeguards, this implementation design offers high upside potential with minimal changes to current procedures.

- **The DAF should adopt a layered test and evaluation strategy.** For implementation designs that stop short of full automation, human performance is still a vital concern. The DAF must adopt a layered test and evaluation strategy that includes systematic testing of

ML models during development, manual testing of human performance, mock boards, A/B testing, and postmortem analysis prior to and after system deployment.

Contents

Figures

Tables

Chapter 1. Introduction

In a letter to the force, Air Force Chief of Staff Gen Charles Brown spoke of a changing global environment that includes aggressive and capable competitors. General Brown emphasized that, to meet this challenge, the Department of the Air Force (DAF) must "recruit, access, educate, train experience, develop and retain Airmen . . . with the attributes required to compete, deter, and win in the high-end fight." He further emphasized that the DAF must "change its decision processes in order to make analytically-informed and timely decisions . . . to enable the USAF [U.S. Air Force] to outpace key competitors' decision cycles" (Brown, 2020).

One way the DAF can transform human resource management (HRM) decision processes is by using analytic methods, such as artificial intelligence (AI) and machine learning (ML). To help HRM decisionmakers apply ML in ways that uphold institutional and societal values, we developed a framework based on the research and business literature on ML safety. In this report, we describe the framework and demonstrate it by applying it to a collection of use cases focused on DAF officer promotion and developmental education (DE) boards. Although we focus on board processes, the principles and techniques that these examples illustrate are applicable throughout HRM.

Background

AI is a discipline concerned with machines demonstrating intelligence—that is, behaving in seemingly rational ways, given what they know (Russel and Norvig, 1995). ML is a subfield of AI that uses statistics to train machines to perform tasks without first providing explicit instruction (Jordan and Mitchell, 2015). Advances in computing power, data availability, and algorithms during the past 15 years have contributed to a surge of interest in AI and have led to many high-profile demonstrations of AI by academia, the government, and private-sector companies (Zhang et al., 2022).

At this point, AI has reached virtually every industry and business function. In a 2021 survey of global executives, 56 percent reported that their company had adopted AI for at least one business function (Chui et al., 2021). Overall, 8 percent of respondents reported using AI to optimize talent management, and 8 percent reported using AI for performance management. AI had significant bottom-line benefits in these use cases. Of the companies that used AI for HRM, 86 percent reported lower costs, and 63 percent reported increased revenue.

Notwithstanding its potential, AI also opens organizations and society at large to new risks. This concern is reflected in the large number of "principles" documents aimed at providing normative guidance for the responsible use of AI (Fjeld et al., 2020). This concern is also reflected in the proliferation of such AI topics as causal effects and counterfactual reasoning, interpretability and explainability, privacy, and fairness and bias that seek to operationalize normative guidance for AI use (Zhang et al., 2022). Collectively, these sources identify and attempt to deal with ways in which AI can violate institutional and societal norms. Moreover, these sources identify ways in which AI can violate federal policies guarding against discrimination based on protected characteristics.

The DAF is positioned to join other government and private-sector organizations in applying AI to all mission areas and support functions, including HRM. The U.S. Department of Defense (DoD) and the DAF have issued the imperative to develop and field AI systems (USAF, 2019; DoD, 2018). In addition, the DAF has created a "fabric" of big-data platforms to curate key information sources and has implemented secure cloud-based business intelligence platforms to enable the development of analytic tools that use those data (Myatt, 2022). These enterprise-level investments create opportunities for the DAF to leverage AI and ML to expand its HRM analytic capabilities. However, as the DAF does so, it must take steps to ensure that it applies ML safely.

Principled Artificial Intelligence

Academic, government, and private-industry interest in AI has exploded since 2010. Figure 1.1 shows the total number of English-language AI publications and patents filed from 2010 to 2021. The number of papers published in 2021 was double the number in 2010. More strikingly, the number of patents filed in 2021 was 55 times greater than in 2010. Nearly all metrics that track the national and global state of AI (e.g., degrees conferred, funding, and job postings) show similar growth over time.

Amid this surge in productivity, AI researchers and policymakers have begun to consider the responsible use of AI. NeurIPS, one of the largest AI conferences, held its first ethics-related workshop in 2014. Since then, NeurIPS has created several workshops around fairness, accountability, and transparency. Figure 1.1 shows that the number of papers published at NeurIPS on these topics in 2021 was seven times greater than in 2015. During the same period, other conferences, such as the ACM (Association for Computing Machines) Conference on Fairness, Accountability, and Transparency, have drawn an increasing number of submissions from academia, government, and industry. These trends reflect mounting awareness that AI may violate institutional and societal norms if it is not used responsibly. Moreover, given the potential harm associated with the human resources context, irresponsible use of AI may violate state and federal regulations.

Figure 1.1. Growth in AI Publications, AI Patent Filings, and Publications on Responsibility

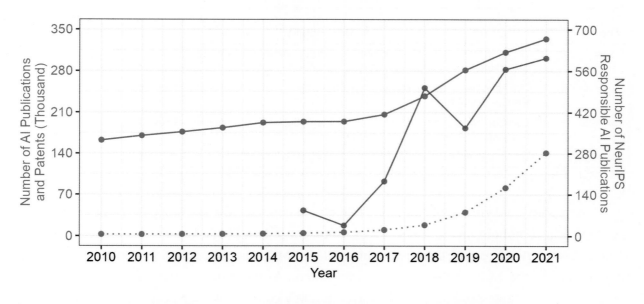

SOURCE: Features data from Neural Information Processing Systems, 2021, and Center for Security and Emerging Technology, 2021.

Table 1.1 lists four themes related to the responsible use of AI from NeurIPS. *Causality* involves understanding the relationship between inputs to AI systems and outputs, such as how demographic variables affect hiring decisions. *Explainability* involves designing AI systems that are interpretable or that can explain their outputs for high-stakes decisions, such as board recommendations. *Fairness* involves ensuring that AI systems do not systematically disadvantage individuals from certain demographic groups—for example, based on race, ethnicity, or gender.[1] Finally, *privacy* involves protecting potentially sensitive personnel information that AI systems may use, such as medical or legal data. The number of publications on these and other safety-related topics has increased rapidly over the past five years.

---

[1] Methods that establish causality can enhance fairness by allowing humans to identify problematic relationships between inputs and outputs, and methods that increase explainability can enhance fairness by allowing humans to understand why an ML system produced a particular output.

Table 1.1. NeurIPS Themes Related to Responsible AI

Theme	Description	Submissions from 2015–2021
Causality	Understanding relationships between inputs and AI system outputs and observing how changing certain inputs affects outputs	284
Explainability	Designing AI systems that can be inherently understood or that can explain their behavior	107
Fairness	Developing AI systems that do not systematically disadvantage individuals from different demographic groups	596
Privacy	Protecting personally identifiable information	483

SOURCE: Features data from Neural Information Processing Systems, 2021.

Along with academia, DoD and the DAF also recognize AI risks and the need to ensure that AI applications uphold institutional values. In response to a 2018 National Defense Authorization Act directive to consider how AI and ML can address national security and defense needs, the National Security Commission on AI identified "aligning systems and uses with American Values and the Rule of Law" as a key consideration. Specifically, AI systems must uphold the constitutional principles of due process, individual privacy, equal protection, and nondiscrimination (National Security Commission on Artificial Intelligence, undated). With this as a guide, the DAF can pursue applications of AI that advance the mission and core values of the USAF and that are consistent with DoD and DAF statements concerning diversity, equity, and inclusion (DAF, 2012; DAF, 2019a; Secretary of Defense, 2020).

The "Iron Triangle" of Accuracy, Fairness, and Explainability

In parallel with the AI boom, there has been a proliferation of policy papers aimed at providing normative guidance for the responsible and ethical use of AI. Based on a review of 36 global principles documents representing private and public sectors, researchers from the Berkman Klein Center for Internet and Society at Harvard University identified eight themes (Fjeld et al., 2020):

1. *Privacy.* AI systems should respect individuals' privacy.
2. *Accountability.* Responsibility for the impacts of AI should be appropriately distributed, and remediation actions should be available.
3. *Safety and Security.* AI systems should perform as intended and should be secure.
4. *Transparency and Explainability.* AI systems should be designed and implemented in a manner that permits oversight.
5. *Fairness and Non-discrimination.* AI systems should maximize fairness across demographic groups.
6. *Human Control.* Important decisions must remain subject to human review.
7. *Professional Responsibility.* Systems must be in place to ensure the professionalism of individuals involved in developing and deploying AI systems.
8. *Promotion of Human Values.* AI means and ends should promote human well-being.

For comparison, the Defense Innovation Board identified five related principles for the ethical development of AI, which should be (1) responsible, (2) equitable, (3) traceable, (4) reliable, and (5) governable; these are reiterated in the DoD Responsible Artificial Intelligence Strategy (Joint Artificial Intelligence Center, 2021; DoD, 2022).

These principles encompass a comprehensive AI strategy that includes how systems are developed and tested, how they are deployed, and how governing bodies regulate the use of AI. From these principles, we extract three concepts that are particularly relevant to evaluating how a system performs in our context: the "iron triangle" of *accuracy*, *fairness*, and *explainability* (Figure 1.2).

Accuracy means that the AI system or the model that it contains correctly predicts the outcome of interest with high probability and aligns with the Defense Innovation Board's definition of *reliable*. *Fairness* means that the AI system treats demographic groups equivalently and aligns with the Defense Innovation Board's definition of *equitable*. *Fairness* can be defined in different ways; for example, it may mean applying the same algorithm to all demographic groups (i.e., procedural fairness), or it may mean that the AI system produces similar outcomes for all demographic groups (i.e., outcome fairness). Lastly, *explainability* means that a human can understand the factors and relationships that led to the AI system's outcome and aligns with the Defense Innovation Board's definition of *traceable*.

Figure 1.2. Iron Triangle of Accuracy, Fairness, and Explainability

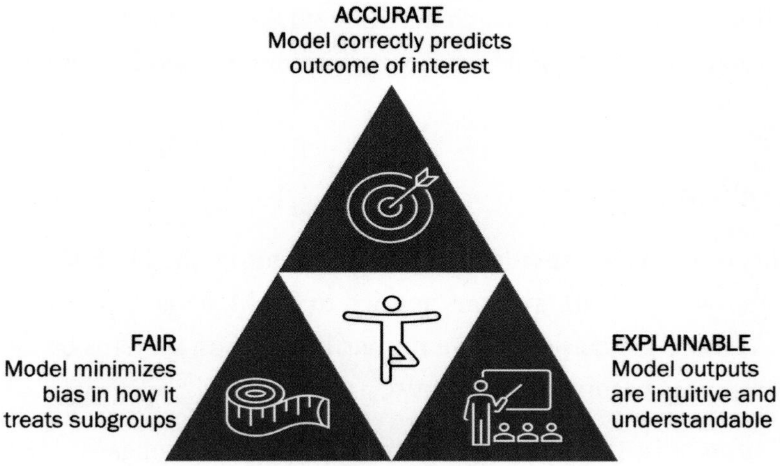

Accuracy, fairness, and explainability may be competing qualities. To increase fairness, system designers may place constraints on the data used to train the model or bound how model outputs are used. These fairness constraints come at a cost. For example, in the judicial context, if an outcome, such as recidivism, is associated with race, blinding the AI system to that variable may reduce its accuracy if suitable measures of the variables that are *causally related* to that outcome are not available. Under these circumstances, forcing the AI system to grant bail to the same percentage of defendants from different racial groups will reduce its accuracy (Corbett-Davies et al., 2017). In the HRM context, blinding the AI system to protected characteristics or forcing the system to grant opportunities to an equal proportion of individuals from different demographic groups may also increase fairness while reducing accuracy.

To increase explainability, system designers may limit model complexity. These complexity constraints also come at a cost. In real-world problems, the relationship between inputs and outcomes is typically multifaceted. ML methods learn "black box" models that approximate these relationships, but in ways that humans cannot readily understand. Simpler models, though more comprehensible, provide lower fidelity approximations of the underlying relationship, and may make less accurate predictions. For example, in the health care context, decision trees may be less accurate than neural networks for predicting clinical outcomes (Caruana et al., 2015). Nevertheless, decision trees may be preferred due to the greater ease of explanation and use by practitioners. In the HRM context, limiting the number of individual attributes and the ways they are combined to predict a career outcome may increase explainability while reducing accuracy.

The principles identified by the Berkman Klein Center for Internet and Society and the Defense Innovation Board make up a comprehensive strategy that includes design, testing, deployment, and governance of AI systems (Fjeld et al., 2020). The term *safety* may be used broadly to encompass all or many of these principles. We choose to define *safety* by the three pillars of accuracy, fairness, and explainability. On one hand, this goes beyond narrow considerations that address only the AI and not the human interaction with the system. On the other hand, other considerations, such as security and the safeguarding of potentially sensitive personal information, are paramount when deciding whether to field a system. In this report, we limit focus to the joint human-machine team's performance without addressing these additional issues.

Organization of the Report

The goal of this report is to provide a framework to allow the DAF to evaluate and provide assurances about the safety of ML systems applied to HRM. Most topics covered in this report are applicable to AI more generally, but we primarily focus on systems capable of learning. The remainder of this report is organized as follows:

- Chapter 2 presents a system design framework that encompasses HRM objectives, ML system implementation designs, and ML system evaluation.
- Chapter 3 presents quantitative and qualitative metrics for evaluating the accuracy, fairness, and explainability of ML systems.
- Chapter 4 presents five potential implementation designs for incorporating ML into board processes.
- Chapter 5 demonstrates how to evaluate the accuracy, fairness, and explainability of ML systems using two examples: officer promotion boards and DE boards.

- Chapter 6 provides guidelines for integrating ML systems with human raters and for evaluating joint human-machine teams.
- Chapter 7 summarizes the main findings and offers recommendations.
- Appendix A presents supplementary safety evaluations for the ML systems described in Chapter 5.
- Appendix B describes a method that shows system designers which potential cutoffs satisfy any desired selection-rate threshold.

Chapter 2. ML System Conceptualization and Design

In this chapter, we present a framework for conceptualizing and designing ML systems for HRM. The framework asks two types of questions about ML system implementation designs. First, is the implementation design useful? Does it satisfy the HRM objective(s) motivating the use case? Second, is the implementation design safe? Does it meet accuracy, fairness, and explainability criteria? To illustrate the motivation behind the framework, we begin by describing the officer promotion and DE process. The use case is meant to be illustrative—the framework is applicable to other HRM use cases as well.

HRM Use Cases

Officer Promotion

The purpose of officer promotion is to select the best-qualified officers for positions of increased responsibility and authority through a fair and competitive process (DAF, 2021). Promotions provide career incentives to attract and retain service members. Further, promotions are essential to meet the current and future needs of the force.

The Defense Officer Personnel Management Act (DOPMA) established military-wide regulations concerning officer promotion, separation, and retirement. DAF officer promotions follow guidelines established by DOPMA and prescribed in Air Force Instructions (DAF, 2021). Officers become eligible for promotion after meeting minimum time in grade (TIG) requirements. All officers who are fully qualified and meet minimum TIG requirements are selected for promotion to O-2 and O-3. The number of officers selected for promotion to O-4 to O-6 annually depends on the projected number of vacancies at the next highest grade.

Career fields are grouped into developmental categories. Competition for promotion is between officers within the same developmental category. Central promotion boards evaluate the records of all officers who are eligible for promotion to O-4 to O-6 and by developmental category. Officers are then selected based on order of merit.

Figure 2.1 gives a high-level view of how promotion boards function (DAF, 2021). The Electronic Board Operations Support System (eBOSS) displays officer selection records (OSRs). For each eligible officer, eBOSS contains a promotion recommendation form (PRF) and officer performance reports (OPRs), documentation of detractors and commendations, and duty history.

Figure 2.1. Field Grade Officer Promotion Board Proceedings

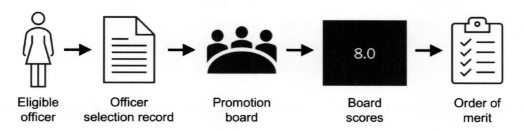

| Eligible officer | Officer selection record | Promotion board | Board scores | Order of merit |

SOURCE: Features information from DAF, 2021.

A promotion board is made up of five to 13 officers senior in rank to those being considered. Board members mirror the characteristics of eligible individuals in terms of race, ethnicity, and gender. Board members review and score each OSR, assigning scores in half-point values from 6.0 (below average) to 10.0 (outstanding). If a board has a significant disagreement about how an OSR should be scored, or a *split* (i.e., a difference of 2.0 points or more between board members), the board reviews the record together, and panel members involved in the disagreement must rescore the record. The final score assigned to a record equals the total of all board members' scores.

Once the records are scored, they are ordered by merit. Based on the promotion quota, an initial cut-line is set above which all records are recommended for promotion. A second cut-line is set one or two score categories below. Records between the cut-lines are said to be *in the gray*. These records are reevaluated with attention to objective negative and positive factors contained in OSRs. The board rescores records that are in the gray to allocate the remaining promotion quota.

Developmental Education

Professional military education (PME) provides broadening opportunities to officers to prepare them for future assignments within and outside their occupational expertise. These opportunities include graduate education, fellowships, experiences with industry, and joint and service PME.

Intermediate Development Education (IDE) is offered to Major selects and Majors (O-4), and Senior Development Education (SDE) is offered to Lieutenant Colonel selects to Colonels (O-5 and O-6) (DAF, 2010). To be eligible for IDE or SDE, the officer must be nominated. Central boards then rate and select from among the nominated individuals. The rules of engagement mirror how promotion boards are run.

Conceptual Framework

Figure 2.2 presents a framework for conceptualizing and designing ML systems for HRM. HRM objectives guide the selection of an ML system implementation design. The implementation design, in turn, affects how the system is evaluated. If the system fails to satisfy accuracy, fairness, and explainability criteria, the implementation design must be modified. If the system still fails to meet these criteria, decisionmakers must consider whether to prioritize other objectives that can be safely met instead. Next, we describe the elements of the framework in turn, using the example of promotion boards.

Figure 2.2. Framework for Selecting and Evaluating ML System Implementation Design

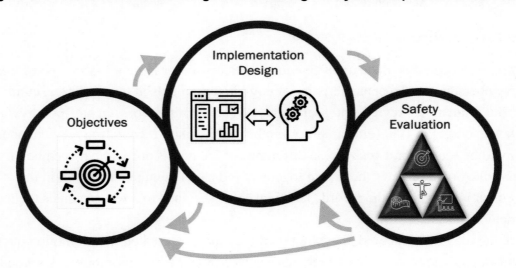

Objectives

AI may be applied to HRM processes to satisfy various business goals. Most basically, the goals can be divided into two categories: using ML to achieve efficiency gains within existing HRM processes versus using ML to enable new HRM processes that provide a competitive advantage (Guenole and Feinzig, 2018). In the case of DAF HRM, these goals map onto executing HRM processes in a cost-effective manner and increasing the effectiveness of HRM processes to field a highly capable workforce.

HRM objectives must be defined at a more granular level to direct ML system implementation design. Table 2.1 shows five HRM objectives that ML systems may satisfy, along with examples linking each to promotion boards. These objectives also apply to DE boards.

Table 2.1. HRM Objectives That ML Systems May Address

Objective	Description	Example from Promotion Board
Reduce workload	An ML system may automatically gather data, generate summaries, and provide recommendations. This may reduce workload, increase efficiency, and optimize the use of human capital by allowing decisionmakers to focus instead on refining machine-generated solutions.	Reduce in-board duration and number of board members needed
Improve human decisionmaking	An ML system may detect relationships between inputs and outcomes that human decisionmakers would otherwise overlook. An ML system may also consider a vast number of solution options. The sensitivity and brute strength of ML systems may allow them to outperform human decisionmakers.	Select best-qualified individuals for positions of increased responsibility and authority
Standardize process	An ML system is not affected by lapses in attention, mistakes, and biases in the ways that human decisionmakers are. Separate from the questions of whether they are accurate or fair, ML systems apply algorithmic methods in a perfectly consistent way across groups and over time.	Increase consistency of outcomes across panels and over time
Advance DAF priorities	Developers may introduce explicit knowledge in the form of rules and constraints, or implicit knowledge in the form of curated sets of training examples, to shape the outcomes of ML systems. This may allow ML systems to immediately optimize different outcomes in a way that human decisionmakers cannot.	Adjust criteria used to generate holistic assessments of individuals in different developmental categories or to reflect institutional changes over time
Increase transparency	AI systems that are inherently interpretable or that can explain their outputs may increase the transparency of decision processes. It may be difficult or impossible for human decisionmakers to fully articulate how they arrived at decisions.	Generate explanations for ML system recommendations
Provide feedback	An ML system may evaluate all officers' records on an annual basis. Using a previously trained model, the system may detect strengths, weaknesses, and gaps and provide developmental feedback to officers.	Identify assignments or development experiences that would increase promotability

Implementation Design

The context of feasible implementations depends on the problem to which the ML system is being applied (Walsh et al., 2021). For instance, command and control problems and HRM problems call for very different ML approaches. Even within HRM, different approaches are needed—for example, to forecast future career field health, to set selective reenlistment bonuses, or to influence officer assignment decisions.

Table 2.2 contains five ML system implementation designs that can enable promotion board processes.[2] All these implementation designs are applicable to other DAF board processes.

---

[2] These implementations are described in more detail in Chapter 4.

Table 2.2. ML System Implementation Designs for Officer Promotion Processes

Design	Description
Decide	The ML system automatically selects individuals for promotion to meet quotas without the intervention of human boards.
Recommend	The ML system places OSRs into three tiers for human boards to use, corresponding with *select*, *evaluate before selecting*, and *do not select*.
Score	The ML system scores OSRs alongside human raters.
Summarize	The ML system generates a summary of the most-significant positive and negative elements contained in an OSR for human boards.
Audit	The ML system predicts promotion outcomes, and the predictions are used to audit the decisions of human boards.

Evaluation

There are two broad categories of measures that we consider when assessing ML-enabled systems for HRM: measures of performance (MoPs) to evaluate whether the system performs as intended, and measures of effectiveness (MoEs) to evaluate whether it leads to the achievement of the process's end goal (Walsh et al., 2021). MoPs and MoEs are related but distinct. For example, an ML system that does not accurately score OSRs has low performance and cannot increase the effectiveness of board processes. An ML system that accurately scores OSRs has high performance, yet it can increase the effectiveness of board processes only if human decisionmakers trust the system enough to use its outputs.

ML models and human raters make up a joint human-machine team (Figure 2.3). MoPs pertain to the behavior of the component parts—the ML model or the human rater—while MoEs pertain to the team's behavior.

Figure 2.3. Measures of Performance and Effectiveness for ML, Humans, and Joint Teams

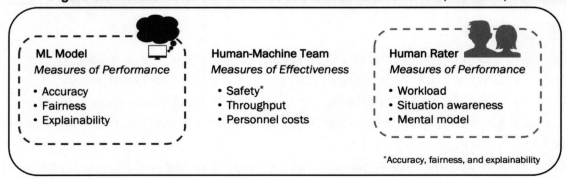

As described in Chapter 1, three criteria for evaluating the safety of the ML model are accuracy, fairness, and explainability. Table 2.3 describes these criteria, along with examples linked to promotion boards. When these criteria are applied to the ML model, they are MoPs.[3] These criteria can also be applied to human raters scoring records without the assistance of an ML model. Table 2.3 describes three additional criteria for evaluating human rater performance: mental workload, accuracy and completeness of the human's mental model of the ML system, and the human's situational awareness (SA) of information that may affect the current decision. Once again, these are MoPs.[4]

The design and performance of the ML system affects human-centered MoPs. For example, an ML system that directs the rater's attention to essential elements of an OSR may decrease workload and increase SA, whereas a poorly calibrated one may actually *increase* workload and *decrease* SA (Parasuraman and Riley, 1997). Additionally, a rater may better understand an ML system that provides explanations along with its recommendations, whereas the rater may form an incorrect mental model for one that does not (Hoffman et al., 2018). The combination of SA and an accurate mental model engenders calibrated trust. In other words, this combination allows humans to trust a reliable ML system but also to anticipate when it is likely to fail, so humans can intervene (Parasuraman and Riley, 1997).

Accuracy, fairness, and explainability can be applied to the human-machine team to assess overall safety. When applied to the team, these criteria are MoEs. Safety depends on ML performance, human performance, and calibrated trust; if human raters trust the ML model but intervene when it is likely to fail, safety of the team will exceed safety of the component parts. Aside from safety, the two primary MoEs are throughput, or efficiency of decisions, and personnel costs, or the amount of human capital needed to conduct the process.

---

[3] We can define *accuracy*, *fairness*, and *explainability* in more ways than the examples provided in Table 2.3. Chapter 3 presents a framework for selecting these criteria and metrics to operationalize ML-centered MoPs.

[4] Chapter 7 describes how to assess human-centered MoPs.

Table 2.3. Criteria for Evaluating ML Applications to HRM

Component	Criterion	Description	Example from Promotion Board
ML model	Accuracy	The ML system predicts the true outcome with high probability.	The ML system predicts board scores that match candidate quality.
	Fairness	The ML system does not systematically disadvantage individuals from different subpopulations.	The ML system does not systematically overpredict or underpredict board scores or promotion likelihoods for individuals from different demographic groups.
	Explainability	A human can understand how the ML system arrived at the predictions or decisions that it did.	A human can understand which factors in the OSR underlie the system's predictions.
Human rater	Workload	The amount of mental demand imposed by a task that can be met by human raters.	By directing attention to key bullets from OPRs, the ML system reduces the human rater's mental workload.
	Situational awareness	The human's recognition and understanding of information that may affect current decisions.	By remaining engaged, the human rater detects push statements, qualifiers, and detractors contained in the current OPR.
	Mental model	The human's understanding of how the ML system operates.	By reading explanations for the ML system's recommendations, the human rater better understands how it operates.
Human-machine team	Safety	The quality of the team's outputs with respect to accuracy, fairness, and explainability.	The human rater combines ML outputs with their own evaluation of records to arrive at more reliable and valid decisions.
	Throughput	The amount of time needed to process a given number of records.	The human rater focuses on information in the OSR highlighted by the ML system, allowing them to evaluate records more quickly.
	Personnel costs	The number of human work hours needed to process a given number of records.	The ML system acts as a surrogate rater, reducing the number of human raters making up the board.

MoEs pertain to whether the system leads to the achievement of the process's overall goals, and so the selection of MoEs to evaluate a joint human-machine team depends on the objective motivating the use case. Regardless, all MoEs are relevant to HRM applications and should be evaluated. Other objectives described in Table 2.1 can be evaluated using a combination of MoEs.

Selection of Suitable Outcome Measures

The framework for evaluating the MoPs and MoEs—or *safety*—of a system is predicated on access to measures that adequately capture the outcome of interest. As described in Volume 2 of this series (Walsh et al., 2024), HRM processes differ in the extent to which their outcomes can be measured. For example, one of the goals of occupational classification is to increase graduation rates from initial skills training. This outcome can be directly assessed. Because *ground truth* (the reality to be modeled with a supervised ML algorithm) is known, statements about the accuracy and fairness of an AI system for enhancing occupational classification are grounded and compelling.

Many HRM processes lack objective outcome measures. For example, one of the goals of promotion is to place individuals with greatest potential into positions of increasing responsibility. Presently, the most direct measure of potential is the judgment of boards of expert human raters. However, these judgments are an imperfect measure of an individual's potential and may be distorted by systematic and nonsystematic forms of error.[5] Because ground truth is not measured in any other way, statements about the accuracy and fairness of an AI system for enhancing board decisions must be understood in the context of the limitations of the available outcome measures.

In this report, we demonstrate the framework using ML-enabled board decisions. The results of the safety evaluation are based on the historical decisions of expert human panels. This is the current standard, though it may be an imperfect measure of an officer's future leadership potential. To evaluate ML (and human rater) performance differently, the USAF could gather additional measures of individuals' performance once promoted.[6]

The principles demonstrated in this report generalize to, and would be strengthened by, the collection of more-direct measures of officer leadership. Likewise, the principles demonstrated in this use case generalize to other HRM processes and are most applicable to processes for which satisfactory ground truth measures exist.

Applying the Framework: ML-Enabled Board Decisions

The first step in using the framework is to ask which system implementation designs meet the objectives motivating the use case. For example, each promotion board is made up of five to 13 officers, in-board time lasts from one to three weeks, and numerous boards are held based on grade and developmental category. This amounts to dozens of work years on an annual basis. If the objective of applying ML to promotion processes is to reduce workload, the most suitable implementation design may be *decide*, which replaces human decisionmaking altogether. Another suitable implementation design may be *summarize*, which allows human decisionmakers to process OSRs more efficiently.

The second step in the framework is to test whether a particular implementation design meets safety criteria—is it accurate, fair, and explainable? For example, the best-suited implementation to reduce workload is likely one that makes promotion decisions automatically. To evaluate such a system, one must ask whether it accurately predicts candidate quality based on the available

---

[5] Suitable measures of ground truth are needed to evaluate a model, and they are also needed to *train* a model. If outcome measures contain systematic errors, a model trained using them may perpetuate historical bias (Kordzadeh and Ghasemaghaei, 2022).

[6] For example, the DAF could retroactively label promotion decisions as correct or incorrect based on individuals' downstream career performance, or based on objective career milestones that some individuals selected for promotion later meet or fail to meet. Such outcomes could provide an alternate measure of ground truth.

outcome measures, whether it performs fairly across different demographic groups, and whether the way that decisions are produced is easy to understand. A system that summarizes OPRs and other data contained in OSRs may also reduce workload, though the savings are less than with a system that automatically decides. In the vast majority of cases, when human decisionmakers are retained, the safety evaluation must also extend beyond the AI system and to the joint human-machine team.

Safety is not an immutable attribute of an ML system. Developers can make design changes to increase an ML system's MoPs and MoEs that will affect the safety. For this reason, the criteria may be applied repeatedly as the system is modified, along with ensuring that the objectives are met. In addition, the accuracy, fairness, and explainability of a system may depend on context—another reason the criteria must be applied repeatedly.

Summary

The defining qualities and attributes of different system implementations determine which HRM objectives the DAF can safely address with ML. Certain implementation designs may be highly effective for meeting HRM objectives, but the DAF should use them only if they can be designed to be accurate, fair, and explainable.

Further, ML systems for HRM are likely to be part of a joint human-machine team. High safety of the ML system is necessary but not sufficient to maximize the overall safety of the human-machine team. Overall safety depends on the performance of the ML model, performance of human raters, and human raters' calibrated trust in the ML model.

Chapter 3. Defining Measures of Performance for Accuracy, Fairness, and Explainability of ML Systems

Chapter 2 introduced a conceptual framework to determine which HRM objectives a system implementation design addresses and whether it does so safely. In this chapter, we discuss ways to evaluate accuracy, fairness, and explainability of ML systems using the example of promotion boards.

Safety Criterion #1: Accuracy

If a model's predictions are not accurate, the model places individuals affected by those predictions at risk. We separate the discussion of accuracy into two parts. First, are the appropriate input data used to train the model? Data problems may degrade model predictions, and so the suitability of the training data must be assessed. Second, how accurate are the model's predictions? There are multiple metrics for assessing accuracy, and choosing the right one depends on how model predictions will be used. We discuss each of these issues in turn.

Defining Accuracy

Accuracy refers to how well the ML model predicts ground truth. As discussed in Chapter 2, choosing outcome measures that reflect ground truth can be difficult in certain contexts; for example, the most-direct measures of ground truth for promotion or development boards are the historical decisions of human experts. In the event that historical decisions suffered from systematic bias or decision error, one might claim that the model is accurate *with respect to the historical decisions*, while it is inaccurate *with respect to the unmeasured bias- and error-free ground truth.*

Prior to evaluating safety, one should consider whether suitable measures of ground truth exist. In cases in which historical data are not available or in which historical data are biased, it may not be possible to make compelling statements about accuracy. This effort can and should be informed by literature on algorithmic bias (Kordzadeh and Ghasemaghaei, 2022).

Evaluating the Appropriateness of the Training Data

Using historical data to train ML models may fail to yield accurate predictions of the future for a variety of reasons (Table 3.1). Broadly, the model may fail because (1) it is unable to infer the relationship between inputs and outcomes from the data that are available, or (2) the relationship between inputs and outcomes has changed in the population since the data were collected. Separately from evaluating model predictions, the training data (i.e., both the predictors and the outcomes) should be evaluated continuously to detect problems that may limit generalizability.

Table 3.1. Criteria for Evaluating ML Applications to HRM

Class of Data Problems	Description	Example
Historical data do not have suitable outcome measures.	The ML model depends on a measure of the target outcome that contains systematic error.	A historical board process was biased against a particular demographic group, and the ML model learns to perpetuate this bias based on language that reveals the protected demographic characteristic.
Historical data do not permit the ML model to learn the underlying relationship between inputs and outcomes.	The ML model places too much weight on factors that are spuriously associated with outcomes (i.e., *overfitting*).	Given the large number of unique duty positions, certain positions will be associated with promotion outcomes by chance. An ML model may learn these spurious associations.
	There are not enough data for the ML model to learn which factors are associated with the outcome (i.e., *underfitting*).	Certain developmental categories contain a small number of career fields and officers, yielding fewer examples for the ML model to learn from.
	The ML model cannot learn which of multiple equally predictive factors is associated with the outcome (i.e., *underspecification*).	The recommendation contained on a PRF is strongly associated with text contained in OPRs and duty history. The ML model learns to use the PRF and ignore all other inputs.
Historical data do not generalize to future use cases.	The inputs have changed over time (i.e., *data drift*).	The form and language used in OPRs has changed from previous versions of the form.
	The relationship between inputs and the outcomes has changed (i.e., *concept drift*).	The DAF has begun to apply tailored criteria to evaluate officers in different developmental categories differently.

Selecting Appropriate Accuracy Performance Metrics

If historical data used to train the model are suitable, the model's predictive accuracy may be assessed. The phrase *predictive accuracy* implies that the model is evaluated on test cases that were not used to train the model. This comes nearest to the real-world challenge of making predictions before the outcomes are known, and it provides an estimate of how well the model will perform in practice.

For the HRM applications we envision, there are two general classes of accuracy metrics (Table 3.2). *Classification metrics* describe how accurately the model assigns cases to different categories (i.e., promotion outcomes), and *regression metrics* describe how accurately the model predicts numeric values (i.e., board scores).

Table 3.2. Criteria for Evaluating Accuracy of ML Applications to HRM

Prediction Task	Metric	Description	Reasons for Use
Classification	Accuracy	Total percentage of cases correctly classified	Equally concerned with incorrect positive classification of individuals and incorrect negative classification of individuals
	Precision	Percentage of positive model classifications that were correct	Concerned with making correct positive classifications
	Recall	Percentage of positive cases that the model correctly identified	Concerned with trying to identify all cases that should be classified positive
Regression	Correlation (r^2)	Proportion of variance in outcomes accounted for by predicted variables	Measures the strength of the relationship between observed and predicted outcomes
	Mean squared error (MSE)	Average of the squared difference between predicted and actual values	More concerned with not making large errors than small errors
	Mean absolute error (MAE)	Average of the absolute difference between predicted and actual values	Concerned with making minimal errors on average for all cases

Safety Criterion #2: Fairness

If a model violates one or more notions of fairness, it may place certain groups of individuals at greater risk. As with accuracy, notions of fairness are applicable only insofar as data meet the previously provided appropriateness standards. Additionally, there must be enough data to train the model, including detecting factors that may uniquely affect individuals in small population segments (e.g., female pilots). Finally, if the data contain bias produced by historical decision processes, the model may learn to perpetuate the same bias. In the following sections, we discuss definitions of *fairness* and corresponding measures.

Defining Fairness

A foundational principle of fairness is that there is no single definition of *fair*—contextual factors, institutional values, and societal norms determine which of an accepted set of *fairness* definitions is most suitable. In all nontrivial cases, it is not possible to satisfy multiple definitions of *fairness*.[7] The implication is that, to evaluate fairness, the DAF must first consider contextual factors related to the specific HRM process, institutional values as expressed in policies and elsewhere, and societal norms. Based on these considerations, the DAF can then choose a relevant definition of *fairness*. Cabreros et al. (2023) provides one set of examples for how DAF policy might be translated into *fairness* definitions.

---

[7] Kleinberg, Mullainathan, and Raghavan (2016) showed that these notions of fairness cannot be simultaneously achieved except in very specific cases. In practice, the institution must choose and justify one measure to optimize for a specific application.

Following the taxonomy used in Cabreros et al. (2023), there are two general classes of fairness. *Procedural fairness* concerns the manner in which the process is administered without respect to its outcomes. For example, blinding decisions to such protected characteristics as race, ethnicity, and gender may increase procedural fairness. The DAF already uses such practices in board processes.[8] However, given that protected characteristics may be inferred from other available information, these practices may not yield complete procedural fairness.

Conversely, *outcome fairness* concerns the process's outcomes and potential differences across groups. Outcome fairness can be exact, or it can allow for a level of tolerated differences between groups (e.g., ensuring that selection rates for men and women differ by 10 percent or less).

Table 3.3 summarizes three generalizable forms of outcome fairness: independence, separation, and sufficiency (Barocas, Hardt, and Narayanan, 2023). *Independence* means that the model predictions, such as *promote* versus *do not promote*, do not differ between demographic groups. This is unlikely to be satisfied in real-world applications because it requires that outcomes, along with factors that influence them, do not differ between demographic groups. For example, suppose we were concerned with fairness between male and female. A model that predicted a higher rate of promotions among male pilots than female pilots would violate the principle of independence.

Separation means that model predictions may differ between demographic groups, but that differences can be accounted for by underlying historical differences. Returning to the previous example, if male and female pilots were promoted at different rates historically, model predictions that reflected that difference would not violate the principle of separation. Like independence, separation is unlikely to be satisfied in real-world applications.

Finally, *sufficiency* means that the true outcome, conditioned on the model's prediction, does not vary by subgroup. For example, if male pilots that the model predicts will have successful careers perform worse than female pilots with equivalent predictions, the model would violate the principle of sufficiency.

---

[8] For example, Air Force Instruction (AFI) 36-2501 tightly governs promotion board proceedings, along with what information about officers may be contained in OSRs (DAF, 2021). Likewise, AFI 36-2406 governs how OPRs are written and prohibits certain types of information related to race, ethnicity, and gender (DAF, 2019b).

Table 3.3. Categories of Outcome Fairness Criteria

Category	Description	Purpose for This Fairness Definition	Can Be Measured by[a]
Independence	ML predictions are unrelated to group identity.	The DAF wants equal selection rates across demographic groups.	Selection rate across groups
Separation	ML predictions are unrelated to group identity after taking true outcomes into account.	The DAF wants equal selection rates across demographic groups after accounting for relevant differences.	Recall across groups
Sufficiency	True outcomes are unrelated to group identity after taking model predictions into account.	The DAF wants model predictions of success to be equally precise across demographic groups.	Precision across groups

[a] Estimates can also be made in the context of regression (Steinberg, Reid, and O'Callaghan, 2020).

Given that ML models trained on historical data do not typically satisfy many definitions of *outcome fairness*, methods can be applied in different stages of ML model development to force a model to satisfy the accepted definition. We do not address these methods in this report. Rather, we evaluate independence and separation for multiple implementation designs while acknowledging that additional methods could be applied to satisfy these definitions of *outcome fairness*.

Safety Criterion #3: Explainability

If an ML system it not explainable, humans may ignore the system or misuse it. The purpose of explanation among humans is to develop a shared mental model of a problem or domain. This improves individual and collective decisionmaking. An additional purpose of explanation among humans is to increase trust. Explanations between ML systems and humans serve the same purposes—to correct and enrich the ML system *or* the human's understanding of the problem or domain, and to engender calibrated trust by the human (Fox, Long, and Magazzeni, 2017). The overarching goal of explanation is to increase the performance of the joint human-machine team.

Explanations may seek to answer many different questions, such as "How does it work?" "What kinds of mistakes can it make?" "Why did it do that?" and "Why didn't it do something else?" Further, different audiences need different types of explanations. For example, in the case of an ML system for promotion boards, (a) senior leaders need explanations that address the legality of the system and that give a general sense of how it arrives at decisions, (b) board members need explanations that allow them to determine when to trust the system and when to intervene, (c) officers who are eligible for promotion need explanations that clarify how the system arrived at the decision that it did for them, and (d) ML engineers need explanations that allow them to diagnose whether and why the system is behaving differently than expected. The implication is that explainability can be assessed only in the context of the end-user's questions and the types of explanations they need.

Defining Explainability

There are two categories of approaches to engineering transparent ML systems (Lipton, 2017; Rudin, 2019). *Intrinsic interpretability* refers to selecting models that make intuitive sense to humans—interpretability is a property of the model. *Post hoc explanation* refers to including additional methods in the ML system to explain its outcomes to humans—explanation is part of the human-machine interface. Intrinsic interpretability and post hoc explanation are not mutually exclusive. An ML system may use an intrinsically interpretable model along with post hoc explanation techniques. However, the need for post hoc explanation is greater if a black box model is used.

Selecting Appropriate Explainable Performance Metrics

Explainability is inseparable from the expectations and thought processes of end-users. Thus, explainability research and metrics for assessing explainability reflect influences of both statistical and social science research methods.

Table 3.4 summarizes transparency metrics that can be applied at each stage of system design (Hoffman et al., 2018; Mohseni, Zarei, and Ragan, 2021).[9] During model selection, one can ask whether the type of model is inherently interpretable.[10] In addition, measures of complexity can be used to compare models from the same family.[11] Measures gathered in this phase are objective and do not require human-in-the-loop testing. However, these measures favor simple models that may not meet accuracy requirements for a given task.

While designing ML system explanations, one can ask whether the explanation meets objective definitions of *good explanations* and whether users are satisfied with explanations (Hoffman et al., 2018). These measures are based on ML experts' and users' responses to Likert-style items about explanations that the ML system provides. Measures gathered in this phase of development can be used to compare any type of ML system. However, these measures require human-in-the-loop testing, which makes them more costly. In addition, humans may favor *persuasive* rather than *accurate* explanations.

---

[9] Doshi-Velez and Kim (2017) presented a taxonomy of interpretability evaluation methods that include functionally grounded, human-grounded, and application-grounded evaluations. The model selection metrics in Table 3.4 are examples of functionally grounded evaluations, the explanation interface metrics in Table 3.4 along with scoring user mental models are examples of human-grounded evaluations, and performance is an example of an application-grounded evaluation.

[10] For example, linear or logistic regression, decision trees, K-Nearest neighbors, rule-based learners, general additive models, and Bayesian models are said to be inherently interpretable (Arrieta et al., 2020). Ensemble models, support vector machines, and neural networks are not.

[11] Measures of complexity are typically used to limit overfitting. *Overfitting* describes a model that fits the training data too well—it learns from true differences and random fluctuations in the training data. Overfitted models generalize poorly to test cases. Reducing model complexity can reduce overfitting, and it can also increase simulatability.

During user integration, one can use knowledge elicitation techniques to determine whether the user has a complete and accurate understanding of the system (Hoffman et al., 2018). This directly addresses the transparency of the ML system. However, it may be very expensive to ask the user about all details of the system's outputs. Alternatively, one can test the performance of the joint human-machine team; do explanations increase throughput and accuracy of decisions? This directly addresses whether the integrated system achieves its purpose. However, it requires costly human-in-the-loop testing.

Table 3.4. Criteria for Evaluating Explainability of ML Applications in HRM

Phase	Metric	Description	Reasons for Use
Model selection	Model type	Whether the ML system uses one of an agreed-upon set of inherently interpretable model types	Determine whether the model is inherently interpretable
	Degrees of freedom	Model-specific measures of complexity	Compare interpretability of two or more models from within same family
Model explanations	Explanation Goodness Checklist	A seven-item checklist to provide an independent evaluation of whether an explanation is good	Determine whether properties of explanations meet standards of good explanations
	Explanation Satisfaction Scale	Likert scales to measure end-users' satisfaction with explanations[a]	Determine whether end-users are satisfied with explanations
User performance	Scoring user mental models	Using knowledge elicitation techniques to understand and evaluate the correctness of end-users' mental models of the ML system	Determine whether end-users accurately understand the ML system
	Performance	Throughput and/or accuracy of joint human-machine team	Determine whether the ML system enhances accomplishment of task goals

[a] For a review, see Hoffman et al., 2018.

Summary

Our synthesis of research on accuracy, fairness, and explainability supports three findings. First, there is not a single metric for accuracy, fairness, or explainability. The choice of metrics for each dimension depends on characteristics of the problem and goals of the institutional process. Second, safety depends on the model, but it also depends on the data that are used to train the model. Finally, safety assessment requires some amount of human-in-the-loop testing. Humans will interact with the outputs of the model in different ways depending on how it is implemented. While we can evaluate this interaction in theory, humans may not always respond in the ways we expect, and this interaction can be better understood through testing.

In the case of accuracy and fairness, ML systems can be directly assessed to screen out early designs; a system that does not meet accuracy or fairness criteria is unlikely to enhance the performance of the joint human-machine team. However, human-in-the-loop testing is still needed to evaluate whether including the ML system increases the safety of the overall process. Explainability depends on the expectations and thought processes of the end-user. Thus, as compared with accuracy and fairness, explainability is even more dependent on human-in-the-loop testing.

Notwithstanding this complexity, ML research provides concrete steps and quantifiable metrics for assessing accuracy, fairness, and explainability. These lessons are applicable to the assessment of ML systems for HRM.

Chapter 4. Application: Determining the DAF Objectives That Different Implementation Designs Meet

Chapter 2 introduced a conceptual framework to determine which HRM objectives an ML system implementation design addresses, along with whether it does so safely. In this chapter, we elaborate on five implementation designs and provide examples of each in the context of officer promotion boards. The examples are not meant to be definitive implementations. Rather, they are starting points to be refined through iterative use of the framework. In addition, these designs generalize to other decisionmaking processes and are readily applicable to other HRM functions that involve convening a board and evaluating personnel records.

In characterizing decision-support systems, Parasuraman, Sheridan, and Wickens (2000) identified ten levels of automation ranging from high (i.e., the computer decides everything and acts without human oversight) to low (i.e., the human decides everything with computer assistance). We order the implementation designs by level of automation.

Implementation Design #1: Decide

The first implementation design is most like people's preconception of how an ML system could be used for promotion decisions (Figure 4.1). In this design, the ML system replaces the human board and automatically makes promotion decisions. The system is trained using historical board outcomes. The model then predicts scores for new officers who are eligible for promotion. The system uses these predictions to sort officers by merit and to set a cutoff to meet promotion quotas.

Figure 4.1. Visual Diagram of the "Decide" ML System Implementation Design

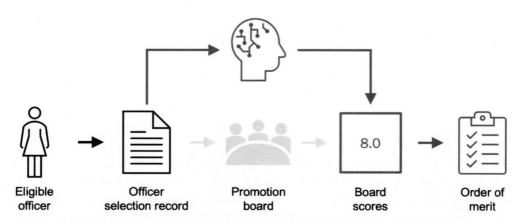

NOTE: Elements in red indicate ML system intervention in the standard promotion board process.

Assessment of Satisfied Objectives

This implementation design significantly reduces workload because human boards no longer convene.[12] It also standardizes the promotion process because the same model is applied to all officers, removing inconsistencies related to rater differences or scoring drift caused by rater fatigue, for example. This does not imply that the ML system will not make errors or that it will not contain bias; its behavior will reflect the historical decisions of human raters used to train it. However, given equivalent records, the system will reach consistent decisions.

This implementation design may increase transparency. Although human board members may have difficulty articulating how they arrived at decisions, the ML system's logic is, in principle, traceable to the underlying model. Information such as input characteristics with high predictive value can be extracted from the model. The implementation design may also help to advance DAF priorities. Because the ML system determines outcomes, the DAF could alter the underlying model or the predictions to produce outcomes consistent with its objectives.[13]

This implementation design does not improve human decisionmaking because it bypasses human decisionmakers altogether. In addition, this implementation design, as described, is not intended to provide feedback to officers.

Implementation Design #2: Recommend

The second implementation design resembles the first in that a model is trained using historical data, and it predicts scores for new officers who are eligible for promotion (Figure 4.2). However, rather than replacing human boards, the system instead provides recommendations to human raters. For example, predicted scores can be used to bin officers into three groups labeled "select," "evaluate before selecting," and "do not select." These approximately correspond to individuals who are well above the first cut-line, in the gray, or well below the second cut-line.

---

[12] All implementation designs introduce a new source of workload in terms of time to create and sustain the ML system. However, this would be more than offset by the staffing savings for some implementation designs.

[13] This could happen in multiple different ways. For simple models, prediction weights given to specific features can be altered. For complex models, feature engineering can be used, or models can be retrained on modified datasets that reflect DAF objectives. In both cases, model outputs can be directly altered. For example, different thresholds can be applied to different demographic groups.

Figure 4.2. Visual Diagram of the "Recommend" ML System Implementation Design

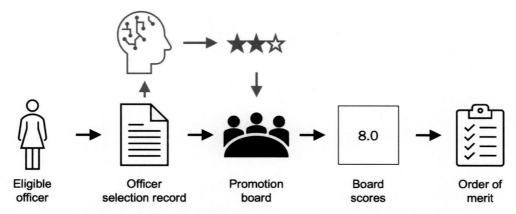

NOTE: Elements in red indicate ML system intervention in the standard promotion board process.

Assessment of Satisfied Objectives

This implementation design reduces workload and improves human decisions by allowing board members to focus time and attention on the subset of records that are most ambiguous with respect to the correct outcome. This implementation design may also standardize the promotion process because the same model is used to generate initial recommendations for all officers. Finally, this implementation design may help to advance DAF priorities because the underlying model or predictions can be modified to generate recommendations consistent with these priorities. However, the ability of this design to standardize processes and advance DAF priorities is somewhat less than for the first design because raters may choose to disregard recommendations.

The implementation design, as described, does not increase transparency or provide feedback to officers. The emphasis is on generating accurate recommendations, which board members may choose to use or ignore.

Implementation Design #3: Score

The third implementation design resembles the first two in that a model is trained using historical data, and it predicts scores for new officers who are eligible for promotion (Figure 4.3). However, rather than providing a recommendation, the machine returns a score on the same scale used by human raters. The machine can be treated as an additional board member, and its score can be included in the total score for the record. Alternatively, the model's score can be used to determine whether a split exists, and to flag and force discussion when human raters deviate significantly from the model's predictions.

Figure 4.3. Visual Diagram of the "Score" ML System Implementation Design

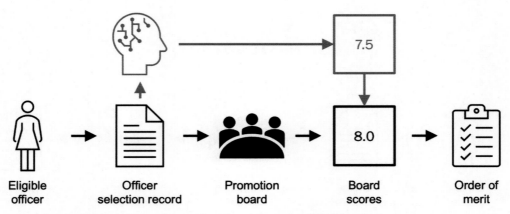

NOTE: Elements in red indicate ML system intervention in the standard promotion board process.

Assessment of Satisfied Objectives

This implementation design primarily standardizes the promotion process because it applies a consistent model to all candidates. This design also advances DAF priorities by allowing system designers to represent those priorities in the scoring model. At a minimum, this will force discussion when board ratings differ from those of the institutionally aligned model. Finally, this design may improve human decisionmaking. By using model scores to flag splits, the implementation design guards against drift that may occur as human raters become fatigued.

The implementation design, as described, does not increase transparency or provide feedback to officers. The emphasis is on generating accurate scores, which may be used to influence board processes (i.e., discussing splits) and board outcomes (i.e., recording scores). In addition, the implementation design does not reduce workload. In fact, it could increase workload if model scores increase the number of splits that the board must discuss.

Implementation Design #4: Summarize

The fourth implementation design is markedly different from the first three (Figure 4.4). Rather than using a model to predict an outcome, this approach provides a concise summary of positive and negative bullets contained in an OSR. To do so, an ML model would once again be trained to reproduce historical outcomes. However, rather than reporting predictions for candidates, the system would summarize the top positive and negative factors that influence each prediction. Model-generated summaries would be provided, along with candidates' records, to the boards. These summaries could also be provided to candidates as a source of formative feedback for career development.

Figure 4.4. Visual Diagram of the "Summarize" ML System Implementation Design

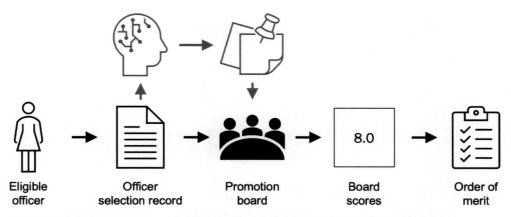

Eligible officer → Officer selection record → Promotion board → Board scores (8.0) → Order of merit

NOTE: Elements in red indicate ML system intervention in the standard promotion board process.

Assessment of Satisfied Objectives

This implementation design primarily improves human decisionmaking by providing concise and accurate information to board members. In addition, this implementation design increases transparency and provides feedback by identifying elements of an officer's OSR that communicate their strengths and weaknesses.

Aside from these primary objectives, the implementation design addresses the remaining four objectives. It may reduce workload by allowing board members to focus on only the most important information with an OSR. However, if the quality of summaries is inconsistent, the design may increase workload. Additionally, it may increase standardization by ensuring that board members attend to "objective" negative and positive quality factors contained in each OSR. Finally, it may advance DAF priorities if these priorities are included in the model used to generate summaries. However, for the implementation design to increase standardization and advance DAF priorities, board members must use information from the summaries it provides.

Implementation Design #5: Audit

In the final implementation design, an ML model is used to audit promotion board outcomes (Figure 4.5). This differs from the previous designs in that it seeks to ensure that promotion board processes are functioning properly rather than trying to influence them. As before, an ML model would be trained to reproduce historical outcomes. The trained model could be used to perform an individual-level audit—that is, flag individuals with high or low predicted promotion probabilities who were passed over or selected, respectively. The trained model could also be used to perform an aggregate-level audit—that is, determine whether overall agreement between human raters and the model exceed a predetermined threshold. Likewise, the trained model could be used to audit results for demographic groups.

Figure 4.5. Visual Diagram of the "Audit" ML System Implementation Design

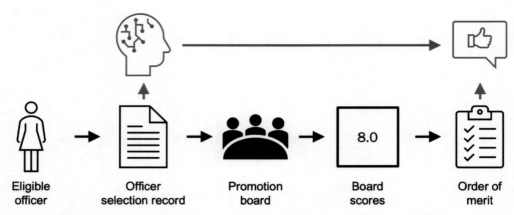

NOTE: Elements in red indicate ML system intervention in the standard promotion board process.

Assessment of Satisfied Objectives

This implementation design may increase transparency and, in the case that board outcomes are substantiated, engender acceptance. Conversely, by auditing outcomes, it may reveal factors that influenced decisions and inform discussions about the potential inaccuracy or unfairness of the process. At the aggregate level, this would standardize promotion processes and ensure that DAF priorities are advanced. At an individual level, this would flag potential errors, thereby improving human decisionmaking. The design would have more-limited benefits in terms of providing feedback or reducing workload.

Comparison of Implementation Designs

Table 4.1 compares alignment to HRM objectives for the different ML system implementation designs. Reading across the rows starting at the bottom, we see that all designs directly or indirectly address the objective of advancing DAF priorities. If the ML system affects promotion outcomes, and if the model that the ML system uses is aligned with DAF priorities, then the ML system can advance DAF priorities. All designs also directly or indirectly address the objective of standardizing processes. If the ML system affects promotion outcomes and if it is applied uniformly across officers, then the ML system will increase standardization of promotion processes. Some, but not all, designs address the objectives of improving human decisionmaking, reducing workload, and increasing transparency. Finally, only one design, *summarize*, addresses the objective of providing feedback. The implication is that the DAF can address some HRM objectives in many ways, whereas the DAF can address only certain objectives through the deliberate selection of a system implementation design.

Table 4.1. Alignment Between System Implementation Designs and HRM Objectives

Objectives	Decide	Recommend	Score	Summarize	Audit
Provide feedback	−	−	−	++	−
Increase transparency	+	−	−	++	+
Standardize processes	++	+	++	+	+
Improve human decisionmaking	−	++	+	++	+
Reduce workload	++	++	−	+	−
Advance DAF priorities	+	++	++	+	+

NOTE: ++ = high alignment; + = moderate alignment; − = low alignment.

Reading down the columns, *summarize* directly or indirectly addresses all HRM objectives. The other system designs each address three or four of the six objectives. The implication is that *summarize* may be most broadly beneficial, while other designs have a specific range of uses.

Summary

A variety of ML system implementation designs can be used to enhance promotion board processes. These designs vary in terms of the HRM objectives they meet and their level of influence and support. This has implications for the risks and benefits that each design entails. Among the five designs we considered, *summarize* addressed all HRM objectives and embodied an attractive risk-benefit trade-off. The next chapter discusses practical applications of the *recommend* and *score* implementations.

Chapter 5. Applied Safety Evaluations of ML Implementations for Boards

In this chapter, we implement and evaluate two system designs. The first involves delivering recommendations for officer promotions, and the second involves providing scores for DE boards. We evaluate the ML models based on accuracy, fairness, and explainability. Our goal is to provide practical examples of how to assess these MoPs rather than to definitively assess the safety of the implementation design.

System Implementation 1: Promotion Recommendations

We trained an ML model to predict O-5 and O-6 promotion outcomes based on text contained in officers' OPRs. For each officer, the model predicts the probability that they will be promoted in a given cycle. We used these probabilities to sort officers by order of merit and to draw cutoffs to predict who will be selected for promotion. The following text box provides a brief methodological summary of data sources and the ML approach we used for the promotion model.

Officer Promotion Model

Model Data
The Promotion Recommendation model takes as input a subset of 205,782 OPRs that the Air Force Personnel Center extracted from the Automated Records Management System (ARMS). ARMS stores officer records as images or portable document format (PDF) files. We extracted the text as described in Schulker, Williams et al. (2024). We combined the data with information from O-5 and O-6 selection boards on whether individuals were selected for promotion.

Model Implementation
We used a combination of natural language processing (NLP) and ML techniques to train models to predict promotion outcomes based on an individual's record. Briefly, this involved (1) extracting text from OPRs, (2) applying standard preprocessing steps to normalize text, (3) converting text to a numerical representation called *term frequency–inverse document frequency* (TF-IDF), and (4) training a regression model on this representation to predict the likelihood of an individual being selected for promotion. The trained model translates each word or phrase in an OPR to a positive or negative change in the odds of being selected.

The figure below contains an example of how the text from an OPR bullet is standardized and decomposed into tokens. The regression model learns a set of coefficients to increase or decrease the odds of being selected based on the tokens contained in a record.

Raw Text

#1 of 19 Sq/CCs! Battle-hardened ldr--flawless cmd record at home & deployed; follow SDE w/JCS and Wg/CC!

Preprocessed and Standardized Text

| #1 | of | <amt> | sq | ccs | battle | hardened | ldr | flawless | cmd | record | at | home | deployed | follow |
| sde | w | jcs | and | wg | cc |

Text Tokenized with Sub-Words

| # | 1 | _of | _19 | _Sq | / | CCs | ! | _Battle | - | hard | ened | _ldr | -- | flawless | _cmd | _record | _at |
| _home | _& | _deployed | ; | _follow | _SDE | _w | / | JCS | _and | _Wg | / | CC | ! |

Model-Generated Summaries
Aside from predicting outcomes, the ML models we trained could be used to identify push statements and detractors contained in OPRs. To do so, the models computed the change in probability when individual bullet statements were replaced by generic text from OPRs. A large upward shift indicates that the bullet has negative valence, whereas a large downward shift indicates that it has positive valence. The figure below shows examples of record-enhancing (left) and moderating (right) text.

Grade	Record Enhancing Text	Record Moderating Text
O-3 (cont'd)	instructor next/groom for WIC	including weekends
	PDE a must	dlvrd 3.1M lbs of fuel to spt 46 TICs
	The mission must be accomplished	
O-2	My #1 of 10 schedulers!	Service Before Self tells us that professional duties take precedence over personal desires
	My #2 of 10 Flt/CCs!	
	It is the moral compass the inner voice	

The primary objectives of this implementation design are to improve human decisionmaking, reduce workload, and advance DAF priorities (Table 4.1). The design can improve human decisionmaking by ensuring that board members observe OPR bullets that, based on historical results, influence promotion outcomes. The design can reduce workload by automating some decisions and by allowing board members to more quickly identify key OPR bullets. Finally, model inputs, model predictions, or the manner in which the model is trained could be altered to advance DAF priorities.

ML recommendations could meet these objectives in a variety of ways. The design we selected involves sorting predicted values and drawing cutoffs to create three separate bins.

- *Select*—officers with the highest predicted promotion probabilities
- *Evaluate before selecting*—officers with intermediate predicted promotion probabilities
- *Do not select*—officers with the lowest predicted promotion probabilities.

By directing human raters' attention to the least-clear records, "Evaluate before selecting," this design reduces workload. Additionally, by allowing board members to allocate greater attention to those records, it improves human decisionmaking. Finally, by including institutional objectives in the ML model that generates recommendations, the design may advance DAF priorities.

The model produces predicting probabilities (between 0 and 1) as output. A key design parameter is where to draw cutoffs of these probabilities to control the number of records given recommendations of either "Select" or "Do not select." Setting conservative cutoffs will give the vast majority of records the recommendation "Evaluate before selecting," increasing rater workload. At the same time, setting conservative cutoffs will increase the performance of the ML model by ensuring that only the strongest and weakest records are labeled "Select" or "Do not select," respectively. And so, the choice of cutoffs controls the trade-off between human workload and ML model performance.

Safety Evaluation

Figure 5.1 shows model predictions for male and female officers and for O-5 and O-6 promotion boards. Bands in blue show the distributions of model predictions for individuals selected for promotion, and bands in red show the distributions of model predictions for individuals not selected for promotion. The vertical dotted line shows the predicted promotion probability for the officer nearest to the cutline.[14] Median predictions for individuals selected for promotion (blue squares) were much higher than predictions for individuals not selected for promotion (red squares).

---

[14] In other words, given the number of vacancies to fill at the next-highest grade, the dotted line shows the predicted promotion probability for the lowest selected officer by order of merit.

Figure 5.1. Distribution of Model Predictions for Officers Selected and Not Selected for Promotion

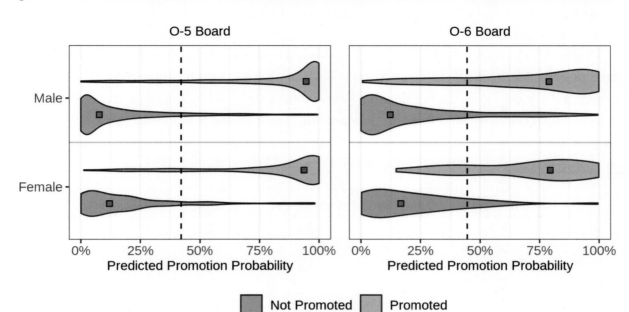

In the following evaluations, we considered a system that issues three types of recommendations: "Select," "Do not select," and "Evaluate before selecting." The recommendation for each officer depends on their predicted promotion probability relative to the promotion probabilities of other officers being considered for promotion.

To start, we ranked all the officers based on their predicted promotion probabilities from the ML model. We identify the predicted probability for the officer in the *Nth* position (depicted by the dotted line in Figure 5.1), where *N* is the quota of available promotions. For a threshold of 10 percent, we recommend "Select" or "Do not select" for the 10 percent of individuals with predicted promotion probabilities furthest from the predicted probability for the officer in the *Nth* position, and "Evaluate before selecting" for the remaining 90 percent of individuals closest to the *Nth* officer.

Put differently, the threshold is used to separate individuals furthest from the cutline, for whom the model's recommendations should be most accurate, from individuals close to the cutline, for whom human judgment is needed. We compared variants of the system with cutoffs of 10, 25, and 50 percent. The intuition is that the model will perform best using a more stringent cutoff (i.e., 10 percent), and it will perform worst when using the most relaxed cutoff (i.e., 50 percent).

Accuracy

To evaluate accuracy, we used the three classification measures from Table 3.2 with one exception; rather than reporting *recall*, which is the percentage of officers actually promoted who were correctly identified by the model, we report the false negative rate (FNR), which is the percentage of officers actually promoted who did not receive a "Select" recommendation.[15] This emphasizes the potentially negative consequences of using an ML model for promotion recommendations.

Table 5.1 shows results for O-5 and O-6 promotion boards. Accuracy, FNR, and precision were highest for the most stringent cutoff (10 percent) and lowest for the most relaxed cutoff (50 percent).[16] By exploring the relationship between the cutoff and model accuracy in this way, decisionmakers can select a value for this parameter that balances workload and risk.

Table 5.1. Accuracy, FNR, and Precision, by Cutoff

Board	Cutoff (%)[a]	Accuracy (%)	FNR (%)	Precision (%)
O-5	10.0	99.4	0.0	99.2
O-5	25.0	98.4	0.5	99.2
O-5	50.0	97.4	1.3	97.9
O-6	10.0	93.2	0.9	95.3
O-6	25.0	92.9	2.1	91.7
O-6	50.0	92.8	4.0	90.5

[a] The percentage of candidates recommended "Select" or "Do not select."

Fairness

To evaluate fairness, we focused on gender. We used *selection rate* (i.e., the percentage of candidates of each gender receiving "Select" recommendations) to measure independence, FNR to measure separation, and precision to measure sufficiency. In practical terms, selection rate measures whether candidates from one gender are more likely to receive "Select" recommendations from the ML model, FNR measures whether equally qualified candidates from one gender are more likely to receive "Do not select" recommendations from the ML model, and precision measures whether candidates who receive "Select" recommendations from the ML model have historically been selected at different rates by human boards. As with accuracy, we considered how these measures vary across three cutoffs.

Table 5.2 shows results for O-5 and O-6 promotion boards. Selection rates were similar between men and women for most cutoffs. As one possible guideline, the 80/20 rule states that relative selection rate for one group should not fall below 80 percent of the selection rate for another (29 CFR 1607.4, 1978). This guideline was violated when the 50-percent cutoff was applied to the O-6 board because selection rate for women was less than 80 percent of what it was for men (16.8 percent versus 21.1 percent). FNR was also similar for men and women. However, when more-relaxed cutoffs were applied, FNR increased more rapidly for female

---

[15] FNR equals 1 minus recall.

[16] Appendix A shows these metrics across all possible cutoffs and how accuracy varies across single-year historical boards.

officers than for male officers. Once again, by exploring the relationship between cutoffs and model fairness in this way, decisionmakers can select a value for this parameter that balances workload and fairness.

Importantly, this relationship between cutoffs and model fairness is not linear. For example, increasing the cutoff does not strictly increase or decrease the relative selection rates between men and women. In Appendix B, we detail a method that shows system designers which potential cutoffs satisfy the 80/20 rule (or any desired selection-rate threshold).

Table 5.2. Precision and Selection Rates Between Men and Women, by Cutoff

Board	Cutoff (%)[a]	Selection Rate		FNR		Precision	
		Female (%)	Male (%)	Female (%)	Male (%)	Female (%)	Male (%)
O-5	10.0	8.5	7.8	0.0	0.0	100	99.1
O-5	25.0	21.0	18.4	0.5	0.5	100	99.1
O-5	50.0	34.8	32.4	1.6	1.3	100	97.7
O-6	10.0	5.2	6.3	0.0	1.1	100	94.9
O-6	25.0	9.7	11.0	2.6	2.1	88.9	92.0
O-6	50.0	16.8	21.1	5.1	3.9	93.3	90.3

[a] The percentage of candidates recommended "Select" or "Do not select."

Explainability

The method used by the ML system, logistic regression, is inherently interpretable in many cases (Arrieta et al., 2020). Additionally, the features used to train the model—words and phrases from OPRs—can be understood by human raters. Moreover, the manner in which the logistic regression model is fitted, by shrinking the values of coefficients for words and phrases that are weakly associated with outcomes, yields a more parsimonious and, hence, more interpretable model. Finally, the addition of an explanation interface that flags the most-significant OPR bullets driving the model's recommendations further increases explainability. For all of these reasons, the ML system has high explainability. However, human-in-the-loop testing would be needed to precisely quantify its explainability.

Failure Modes

This implementation design has two primary failure modes. First, the implementation depends on human raters trusting recommendations. Using an ML model that is inherently interpretable and includes an explanation interface engenders trust that will make acceptance of the recommendations more likely. However, human raters would also require training, education, and experience to develop trust. The implementation fails if the humans do not accept the recommendations as provided.

Second, the implementation depends on the selection of a suitable cutoff and, hence, the number of recommendations for "Select" and "Do not select." Using more-conservative cutoffs increases the accuracy and fairness of the ML model, but at the expense of rater workload, by reducing the number of directive recommendations. Using more relaxed cutoffs reduces rater workload by increasing the number of directive recommendations, but at the expense of model accuracy. By calculating accuracy and fairness metrics, the USAF can explore the trade space within this implementation design and compare it with other implementation designs for giving promotion recommendations.

System Implementation 2: DE Scores

We trained an ML model to predict IDE and SDE board scores based on text contained in officers' OPRs. The approach was exactly the same as for the promotion model, except that the outcome being predicted, a board score, ranged continuously from 6 (lowest) to 10 (highest). The primary objectives of this system implementation design are to standardize processes and to advance DAF priorities (Table 4.1). ML scores could be used in a variety of ways to meet these objectives. The design we selected involves combining the ML score with human ratings. This is akin to a "machine on the board." By applying a scoring algorithm in a consistent manner across all boards and individuals, this design increases standardization. Additionally, by including institutional objectives in the ML model that generates scores, this design may advance DAF priorities.

A key design parameter is the amount of weight given to the ML score relative to human ratings. Lowering the weight will reduce the model's influence, and increasing the weight will reduce humans' influence. And so, the choice of weight controls the trade-off between standardization and rater influence.

Safety Evaluation

Figure 5.2 shows model predictions for male and female officers and for IDE and SDE boards versus human rater scores. Predictions were positively associated with rater scores, but they were also less variable. In other words, the model underpredicted values for officers with the highest IDE and SDE scores and overpredicted values for officers with the lowest IDE and SDE scores. For example, when raters scored records 7 or below, the model predicted scores in the range of 7 to 8. Alternatively, when raters scored records 9 or above, the model predicted scores in the range of 8 to 9.

Figure 5.2. Distribution of Model Predictions for Officers Selected and Not Selected for Promotion

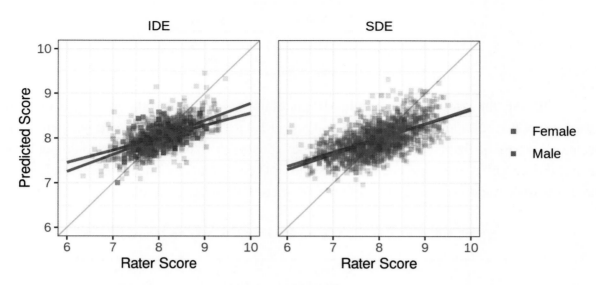

In the following evaluations, we compared ML predictions with historical board scores. To illustrate the effects of combining ML predictions with human ratings, we computed combined scores that gave varying levels of weight to the ML model: 0.1, 0.5, and 1.0. For example, in the first case, the combined score equaled 0.1 multiplied by the model prediction plus 0.9 multiplied by the average human rater score. In the third example, the combined score gave all weight (1.0) to the model prediction, effectively automating decisions.

Accuracy

To evaluate accuracy, we used the two regression measures from Table 3.2: percentage of variance accounted for and MAE. The models accounted for about 36 percent of variance in scores for IDE and SDE boards.[17] Table 5.3 shows MAE between model predictions and actual scores for IDE and SDE boards. MAEs were somewhat greater for SDE because of the larger range of board scores in that case. For comparison, we computed the MAE between records of officers selected for IDE or SDE versus ones who were not. If model error approaches or exceeds the difference between these groups, it would indicate that the model is not accurate enough to reliably score records. MAEs for model predictions were roughly half the size of the average difference between the scores of officers selected for IDE or SDE versus ones who were not. This level of error suggests that the model may not be accurate enough to reliably distinguish between officers who were and were not selected.

---

[17] Based on the R-squared measure for model fit.

Table 5.3. MAE for IDE and SDE Board Model Predictions

Board	Model	Selection
IDE	0.35	0.63
SDE	0.39	0.86

To illustrate the effects of combining ML predictions with human ratings, we recomputed board scores after assigning weights of 0.1, 0.5, and 1.0 to ML predictions, and we identified decision reversals—that is, the percentage of individuals selected for DE who would not have been if the weighted score had been used instead.[18] The percentage of decision reversals increased with model weight, and more for SDE than IDE boards (Table 5.4).

Table 5.4. IDE and SDE Decision Reversals Based on Model Weight

Board	Model Weight	Overall Decision Reversals (%)	Female Decision Reversals (%)	Male Decision Reversals (%)
IDE	0.1	1.6	2.6	1.4
IDE	0.5	11.3	14.5	12.0
IDE	1.0	27.3	36.8	25.1
SDE	0.1	2.6	0.0	2.91
SDE	0.5	17.1	20.6	16.7
SDE	1.0	41.9	47.1	40.7

Fairness

To evaluate fairness, we again focused on the difference between men and women. In the case of regression, the fairness metrics were less intuitive than those we saw with classification in the promotion board example. We computed measures for the three categories of fairness defined in Chapter 3 (Steinberg, Reid, and O'Callaghan, 2020). A ratio of 1 indicates parity between men and women. The values for all three fairness metrics for IDE and SDE boards were close to this value, suggesting that the model performs similarly for both men and women. Table 5.5 shows results for IDE and SDE boards.

---

[18] This assumes that selection occurs by taking those with the top scores and does not account for gray zone selections.

Table 5.5. Fairness Metrics Between Men and Women

Board	Independence Ratio	Separation Ratio	Sufficiency Ratio
IDE	1.03	1.03	1.11
SDE	1.01	1.02	1.01

Explainability

Human raters do not need to understand model predictions in this use case because the ML predictions are appended to board scores after the fact. Nonetheless, the ML model must be explainable for policymakers to adopt it in the first place. Once again, the method used by the ML system (penalized linear regression) is inherently interpretable and yields parsimonious models, the words and phrases from OPRs that the model uses to make predictions can be understood by subject-matter experts, and the explanation interface allows subject-matter experts to confirm the model's behavior. For all of these reasons, the ML system has high explainability.

Additionally, as discussed in Chapter 4, this implementation could be used to flag splits between the ML scores and the human raters. In that case, raters would need to understand individual predictions to know why the ML score differs from their scores. The inherently interpretable nature of the model and methods, along with the explanation interface, contribute to explainability.

Failure Modes

The primary failure mode for this design is for the ML model to make inaccurate predictions. Indeed, the model did not capture the full amount of variation present in human scores. This suggests that more data or a different modeling approach is needed to meet the accuracy criterion. Using a model that does not meet accuracy standards may introduce noise or, worse yet, systematic error.

If model predictions were compared to rater scores and used to flag splits, another potential failure mode is for the model to trigger too many reviews, increasing rater workload. This may occur if the threshold for flagging splits is set too low, or if mode predictions are inaccurate.

Summary

The examples in this chapter show how ML models can recommend promotion outcomes and provide DE board scores. In these ways, ML models can satisfy multiple HRM objectives; specifically, reducing rater workload, standardizing board processes, and advancing DAF priorities. However, if the ML models are not properly evaluated, they may fail to satisfy these objectives, and they risk disadvantaging certain individuals and groups.

We found that the promotion recommendation design traded off accuracy for workload savings. By specifying an acceptable level of model accuracy, the DAF could set the percentage of recommendations to issue while managing risk. The DE scoring design did not meet accuracy standards, but it potentially could if more data from DE boards were available.

The promotion recommendation design violated some fairness standards for certain values of the cutoff. The DE scoring design did not directly violate fairness standards. However, if model predictions were combined with rater scores, this could lead to more decision reversals (potentially positive and negative) for female officers.

Finally, both designs require that decisionmakers and frontline workers understand and trust the ML model. The design choices and manner in which the model was trained and used make it more inherently interpretable and allow its predictions to be explained.

Chapter 6. Human-Machine Integration and Testing

In Chapter 5, we evaluated MoPs for two ML models—one for giving promotion recommendations and the other for predicting IDE and SDE scores. In many applications, model outputs will be provided as inputs to human raters. In this chapter, we shift focus to MoPs for human raters, who must incorporate ML outputs into their decisionmaking. After discussing possible human failure modes, we turn to evaluating MoEs of the joint human-machine team.

The framework illustrated in Figure 2.2 primarily pertains to the safety of the *AI system*. Safety of the AI system is necessary, but not sufficient, to ensure safety of the joint human-machine team. This chapter advances ideas on how to ensure safety of the joint team.

Performance of Human Raters with Model Integration

Cognitive Analysis of Implementation Designs

Parasuraman, Sheridan, and Wickens (2000) proposed a multistage model of task performance that includes (1) acquiring and filtering information, (2) analyzing information, and (3) reaching a decision based on information. ML-informed decision-support systems may provide varying degrees of support across each of these stages, ranging from fully autonomous to fully manual.

Reliable decision-support systems *reduce workload* across all stages by reducing the number of inputs for humans to consider, by extracting critical information from inputs prior to the point of decision, or by recommending suitable decisions as a starting point. Reliable decision-support systems may also *increase SA* across the first two stages by helping humans to focus attention on the most critical inputs and to make sense of them.[19]

Conversely, unreliable decision-support systems may *increase workload* across all stages of task performance by causing individuals to focus on irrelevant information, by forcing them to consider results from incorrect analyses, or by giving them inconsistent recommendations. In addition, poor decision-support systems may *reduce SA* with misplaced complacency—that is, the failure of humans to monitor information sources beyond the outputs of the ML model. In the case of an unreliable decision-support system, this may lead to failure to intervene when the system is incorrect.

Table 6.1 shows the level of support across the stages of human task performance for each implementation design. *Decide* has the greatest potential to reduce workload if it is reliably

---

[19] Reliable systems that make decisions may cause complacency by allowing humans to disengage from the process, which is problematic in rare cases when autonomy fails. This is sometimes called the *lumberjack effect*—the more reliable the autonomy, the harder the fall when it fails.

implemented. However, it also presents risk in terms of complacency, since it may remove the human from the decision process. Because *audit* is applied after boards convene, it does not affect workload, SA, or complacency.[20] *Recommend, score,* and *summarize* may reduce workload and increase SA during information acquisition and analysis. In addition, they are less likely than *decide* to cause complacency and so may reflect an attractive trade-off between the benefits and risks of decision-support systems. Finally, these designs require that human raters continue to exercise judgment and decisionmaking, so these designs may minimize skill decay.

Table 6.1. Level of Automation Across Information Processing Stages

Information Processing Stage	Decide	Recommend	Score	Summarize	Audit
Information acquisition	High	Moderate	Moderate	Moderate	Low
Information analysis	High	Moderate	Moderate	Low	Low
Decision selection	High	Low	Low	Low	Low

Regardless of the implementation design selected, the application of AI to board processes drives the need for new education and training. To interact with the system properly, end-users must understand potential issues, both technical and nontechnical, affecting its use. In this sense, training and education can complement the use of intrinsically interpretable methods and post hoc explanations to increase understandability.

Model Explanations

In Chapter 5, we evaluated ML model recommendations and scores given as outputs to human raters. Here, we consider explanations as another type of model output. The explanations our system generates summarize the most-positive or -negative statements contained in the OPR, as judged by the model, for human raters.[21] Providing these explanations can meet several objectives: principally, to increase a human rater's SA of information contributing to the ML system's decisions, to improve the rater's mental model of how the ML system uses that information, and to engender calibrated trust in the ML system. The model description in Chapter 5 illustrates how the model provides explanations.

Notwithstanding the potential benefits of explanation, the summaries given to human raters could also lead to new failure modes. First, raters may become overly reliant on summaries. Even if raters read beyond the model's output, bullets contained in the summary may produce a priming effect. For example, if the summary mentions a Letter of Reprimand from early in an individual's career, raters may judge the individual more harshly even if the officer has since addressed the behavior. Relatedly, although references to such legally protected demographic

---

[20] An audit system could actually incentivize *less* complacency.

[21] This is also an example of the *summarize* approach described in Chapter 4.

characteristics as race, gender, and ethnicity are prohibited in OPRs, indirect references, such as attendance at a historically black college or university, may introduce the possibility of an undesirable degree of disparate treatment for candidates of different backgrounds.

Second, ML models are often incapable of interpreting nuance. Thus, poorly calibrated model summaries may cause raters to lose trust in ML systems or, worse yet, to incorrectly interpret bullets contained in OPRs. For example, stratification statements are generally positive, but different types of stratification carry different weights. An unqualified stratification statement (e.g., "#1/10 Capts") is stronger than a qualified one (e.g. "#1/10 Capts *as company grade officer of the qtr*"). Certain models would treat these statements equivalently, whereas seasoned human raters would recognize the first statement as being stronger. Human-in-the-loop testing is needed to detect and correct for these failure modes.

Test and Evaluation of Integrated Human-Machine Team

The ultimate concern for the DAF is whether including variants of ML systems, such as ones that provide recommendations, scores, and summaries, improves the overall effectiveness of the joint human-machine team. What are the net effects in terms of decision quality, throughput, and human capital needs? To address these MoEs, the DAF must apply a test and evaluation strategy that encompasses development test and evaluation (DT&E) and operational test and evaluation (OT&E).

Development Test and Evaluation

The DT&E strategy for ML-enabled boards can leverage automated testing of MoPs for the ML model and manual testing of MoPs for human raters.

As the system is developed, testing may be performed to ensure that it meets technical specifications. The evaluations reported in Chapter 5 are examples of DT&E; they demonstrate the performance of ML models using historical records and board results. These records can be included as part of an automated testing strategy for evaluating the technical performance of ML models.

An automated test strategy for explainability is less clear. In the case of summaries provided by our ML models, trained board members could manually identify influential bullets from a collection of OPRs and code their valence. Model summaries could be automatically evaluated, then, based on the extent to which critical features identified by the model overlap with those identified by subject-matter experts.

Human-centered MoPs (workload, SA, and mental models) require human-in-the-loop testing. In the DT&E stage, this testing could occur using non–board members under controlled, laboratory conditions.

Operational Test and Evaluation

The OT&E strategy for ML-enabled boards can leverage mock boards, A/B testing, and postmortem analysis. Prior to introducing significant policy changes, the DAF already conducts and analyzes results from mock promotion boards. Likewise, the DAF could use mock boards to perform OT&E of human-machine teams in a realistic operational environment and with true board members.

The basic design for a mock board for performing OT&E of a human-machine team could resemble the following. A predetermined number of O-6 records are selected. In the *control condition,* a board made up entirely of humans evaluates and assigns scores to the records. In the *treatment condition*, an ML system delivers recommendations and summaries to humans, who once again evaluate and assign scores to the records. For both conditions, decisions and time are recorded.

Time can be converted to *throughput* (i.e., the number of records that can be scored in a fixed amount of time and with a fixed amount of raters) or *human capital needs* (i.e., the number of raters needed to score a fixed number of records in a fixed amount of time). In this way, it is possible to compare throughput and human capital needs between the control and treatment conditions.

Decision quality is more difficult to assess. If the control and treatment conditions score the records similarly, but the treatment condition does so more quickly, this means that the ML system increases throughput without affecting accuracy. If the scores differ, it is not clear whether the control or treatment condition has higher decision quality. To overcome this limitation, OT&E could be conducted using a subset of O-6 records previously scored by a large number of expert raters and with high consensus.

Another tool available at this stage is *A/B testing*. This is a user experience methodology that involves comparing the behavior of users randomly assigned to one of two different variants of a system. The outcome of interest (e.g., decision quality or throughput) is then compared between groups. To use A/B testing to evaluate a new ML-enabled design, the DAF can take advantage of the fact that each board is made up of multiple raters. During board proceedings, each rater can be randomly assigned to the *treatment condition* for a subset of records. The remaining raters, who score the same records but without the assistance of an ML model, form the *control condition*. The performance of the treatment and control groups can be compared and, given the high-stakes nature of decisions, the scores from the treatment condition can be omitted from the final scores given to candidates.

The final tool available for OT&E is postmortem analysis of board decisions. The DAF already analyzes board results to examine how scores vary by personnel subgroup and to identify the factors most strongly associated with board outcomes. The DAF should continue to do so for human-machine teams. However, a complicating factor is that to go beyond descriptive analyses, the DAF would need to operationalize what it means for a board to function properly. This could be based, for example, on maintaining consistency with historical trends, or by using future performance measures and career outcomes of those selected. Another complicating factor is that once the new process is in place, it influences the future data that can possibly be gathered. Future career outcomes are known only for individuals who are selected.

Including humans in the decision process somewhat decouples the ML model from the data that are collected, given that human raters will sometimes go against the model. Outcomes from these cases may continue to provide an important learning signal to the model. In addition, even after an ML model is adopted, the A/B design can be used to continuously compare human-machine teams to raters without the assistance of the ML model and to generate training signals not contaminated by machine outputs.

Summary

As part of joint human-machine teams, raters must incorporate information from ML models into their decisionmaking. Inputs from ML models have the potential to improve human decisionmaking by enhancing information acquisition and processing. However, if the ML systems are not properly tested, they may impair human decisionmaking even if the models themselves perform well in isolation. To address human performance and the effectiveness of joint human-machine teams, the DAF must adopt a testing strategy that includes DT&E and OT&E, that begins as the ML system is being developed, and that remains in place even after the system is deployed.

Chapter 7. Summary and Recommendations

As the DAF undertakes applying ML to HRM, it must take care to ensure that it does so safely. This is in line with the five principles for the ethical development of AI identified by the Defense Innovation Board—responsible, equitable, traceable, reliable, and governable—and with the six tenets contained in the recently released DoD Responsible Artificial Intelligence Strategy (DoD, 2022). To comply with DoD guidelines and ensure that applications of ML uphold institutional values, the DAF must ensure that ML systems are accurate, fair, and explainable.

This research supports the following conclusions, each with recommendations for the DAF HRM enterprise to consider as it seeks to encourage wider adoption of ML in the HRM domain.

Conclusion 1: To Be 'Safe,' ML Systems for HRM Must Be Accurate, Fair, and Explainable

ML research tends to place undue emphasis on accuracy. This narrow view may lead to unsafe, inequitable, and inexplicable outcomes in applying ML to HRM. Fairness and explainability must be considered alongside accuracy to ensure that ML systems are safe.

Recommendation 1a: Settle on Application-Specific Definitions of Accuracy, Fairness, and Explainability

There are not universal definitions of *accuracy*, *fairness*, or *explainability*, and satisfying one definition does not ensure that the ML system satisfies others. For example, *fairness* may mean that the ML model produces equal outcomes for different demographic groups, or that the differences in its outcomes can be accounted for by other factors that differ between groups. Before evaluating an ML system, the DAF must settle on application-specific definitions for *accuracy*, *fairness*, and *explainability*. The DAF may then select metrics based on these definitions.

Recommendation 1b: Determine the Relative Importance of Each Dimension for a Given Application

Accuracy may compete with fairness and explainability. For example, to increase fairness, system designers may prevent models from learning relationships between protected characteristics and outcomes. Likewise, to increase explainability, system designers may use more-interpretable but less-flexible modeling approaches. Before evaluating an ML system, the DAF must determine the relative importance of accuracy, fairness, and explainability for the given application.

Conclusion 2: Evaluation of an ML Model Is Inseparable from Its Objectives and Implementation Design

The framework shown in Figure 2.1 involves stating HRM objectives motivating the use case, identifying an ML implementation design to meet those objectives, and selecting and applying evaluation metrics to ensure that the system is safe. The way in which an ML model is implemented may need to be adjusted to satisfy safety criteria. Changes to the way the ML model is implemented, in turn, may affect its ability to meet the HRM objectives motivating the use case.

Recommendation 2a. The DAF Should Use This Framework to Select, Design, and Evaluate ML Systems

The framework embodies two principles that the DAF should adhere to when applying ML to HRM. First, set the final tests in advance (i.e., safety and effectiveness), and build the system to the tests. Second, incrementally refine the system as it is tested to balance the trade-off between safety and effectiveness.

Conclusion 3: The DAF Can Apply ML to Board Processes in Different Ways

Perhaps the most obvious way to apply ML to board processes is to replace human raters. However, there is a range of alternatives that stop short of full automation. For example, an ML model can recommend decisions, summarize records, or audit outcomes. These designs are aligned to different HRM objectives, and they satisfy different safety criteria.

Recommendation 3a. Before Implementing ML Models, the DAF Should Specify the HRM Objectives Motivating the Application

An ML model applied to board processes can meet one or more objectives, such as standardizing processes, improving human decisionmaking, or reducing workload. Different objectives call for different implementation designs. Thus, the specification of objectives should come before the choice of an implementation design.

Recommendation 3b. The DAF Should Moderate the ML System's Influence to Control the Trade-Off Between Business Value and Risk

The implementation designs we considered can be scaled to increase or decrease the influence of the ML model to outcomes—for example, by varying the number of recommendations issued by the model or by changing the weight assigned to model scores. Besides selecting implementation designs to meet different HRM objectives, the DAF should scale these designs to balance business value and risk.

Recommendation 3c. The DAF Should Follow an Implementation Strategy That Involves Applying ML to Limited Cases Before Gradually Expanding in Scope and Consequence

The DAF does not face a binary decision with respect to the question of whether to use ML for HRM. If a particular implementation is deemed too risky, the DAF may select from potentially less potent but safer designs. This can be achieved by selecting systems that meet different HRM objectives (Recommendation 2a), or by scaling the implementation (Recommendation 2b). Although initial use cases may not meet the DAF's full ambitions, they provide a starting point for ML adoption.

Conclusion 4: Among the Designs Considered, Generating Automated Summaries of Narrative Text Contained in Evaluations Is Extremely Flexible

Of the various ways to employ AI for board processes, the capability to summarize narrative text is not the most obvious application. Yet this implementation design has moderate or high alignment with all HRM objectives (Table 4.1), is unlikely to cause complacency in human raters (Table 6.1), and can be used as a stand-alone system or as an explanation interface for other implementation designs. For all these reasons, *summarize* is a high-leverage implementation design.

Recommendation 4a. The DAF Should Continue to Invest in an ML Capability to Automatically Summarize Narrative Performance Evaluations

In companion volumes to this report, we demonstrate the feasibility of using standard NLP methods to extract information from narrative descriptions contained in performance evaluations. Given the utility of this implementation design, the DAF should build on this proof-of-concept and compare it with systems that use other state-of-the-art NLP approaches.

Recommendation 4b. The DAF Should Conduct User Testing with a System That Summarizes Narrative Performance Evaluations

Unlike the other implementation designs, which produce recommendations or scores that can be compared with historical board outcomes, the quality of summaries depends on how well they meet operators' needs. To advance this implementation design, the DAF must conduct user testing to determine *what* summaries must contain, *how* information must be presented, and *whether* users find the outputs to be useful. Such testing is critical to ensure the safety of these summaries (as discussed in Chapter 6), to help users develop calibrated trust, and to reduce the potential for misuse of system outputs.

Conclusion 5: Evaluation Must Extend Beyond Research and Development of the ML Model

For implementation designs that stop short of full automation, human performance is still a vital concern. Although it is essential to evaluate the ML model, the safety evaluation is incomplete without a human in the loop.

Recommendation 5a. Perform Systematic Testing of ML Models During Research and Development

Model accuracy and fairness are necessary to increase the effectiveness of a joint human-machine team. Using historical data, model accuracy and fairness can be evaluated during DT&E in a systematic and objective manner.

Recommendation 5b. Perform Manual Testing of Human Performance

Model accuracy and fairness are necessary but not sufficient to increase the effectiveness of a joint human-machine team. Thus, in addition to evaluating model accuracy and fairness, system designers must evaluate how different ML models affect human rater workload, SA, and mental models during DT&E.

Recommendation 5c. Adopt a Layered Test and Evaluation Strategy That Extends Forward in Time

Besides measuring the performance of the components of the human-machine team—human raters and ML models—the DAF must adopt a test and evaluation strategy that allows for ongoing OT&E. A layered strategy may include such tools as mock boards, A/B testing, and postmortem analysis of board outcomes. Besides providing markers of whether the implementation design is safe, these evaluations reveal whether it is meeting its objectives.

Appendix A. Supplementary Safety Evaluations for ML Systems

In this appendix, we report supplementary safety evaluations for the ML systems described in Chapter 5.

System Implementation 1: Promotion Recommendations

Accuracy

In Chapter 5, we reported safety metrics for three values of recommendation cutoffs (10 percent, 25 percent, and 50 percent). Figure A.1 shows FNR and precision for all cutoffs ranging from 1 to 100 percent for O-5 recommendations. Values to the left correspond to fewer automated recommendations, and values to the right correspond to more automated recommendations. As the percentage of automated recommendations increases, *FNR* (i.e., the percentage of officers actually promoted who received a "Do not select" recommendation) increases, and *precision* (i.e., the percentage of officers who received a "Select" recommendation who were actually promoted) decreases. This reflects the fact that, as the percentage of automated recommendations increases, the model must distinguish between more-ambiguous records. The DAF can use this type of analysis to determine a value for the cutoff to meet the accuracy criterion.

Figure A.1. FNR and Precision for Model Recommendations for O-5 Promotions, by Cutoff

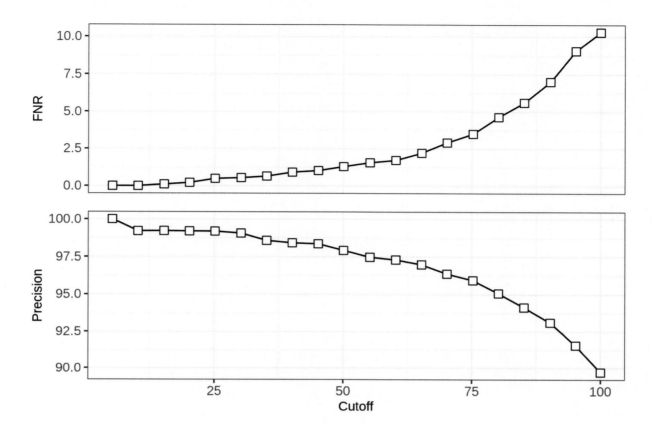

Our assessment of accuracy combined information across multiple boards. By measuring accuracy by individual board, it is possible to show how much accuracy may vary from year to year. It is also possible to determine whether the model's performance has a time trend, which may suggest that the model is biased by temporal distribution shifts in the training data.

Table A.1 shows accuracy, FNR, and precision for O-6 boards, by year. Accuracy was somewhat lower in 2019, although this does not appear to be part of a larger trend. However, accuracy should be monitored in future years to ensure that it returns to historical levels.

Table A.1. Accuracy, FNR, and Precision for Model Recommendations for O-6 Promotions, by Year

O-6 Board	Cutoff (%)	Accuracy (%)	FNR (%)	Precision (%)
2012	10	100.0	0.0	100
2014	10	100.0	0.0	NA[a]
2015	10	86.4	0.0	86.4
2016	10	100.0	0.0	100
2019	10	75.0	4.5	NA[a]
2012	25	95.2	0.0	93.2
2014	25	100.0	0.0	NA[a]
2015	25	94.5	0.0	89.3
2016	25	97.4	0.0	96.7
2019	25	71.8	10.2	71.4
2012	50	94.4	2.1	90.7
2014	50	96.5	4.2	95.2
2015	50	94.5	1.1	89.4
2016	50	94.8	1.2	92.9
2019	50	80.8	11.4	86.4

[a] A precision value of NA implies that no candidates received the "Select" recommendation because none was clearly distinguishable from the gray zone. All candidates who received automated recommendations in this scenario received "Do not Select."

Fairness

As with accuracy, we computed fairness metrics for cutoffs ranging from 1 to 100 percent for O-5 recommendations (Figure A.2). As the percentage of automated recommendations increases, female offices are selected at a higher rate than male officers. The FNR for female officers is somewhat lower for cutoffs below 80 percent, after which it reverses. Finally, precision is higher for female officers across all values for the cutoff.

Figure A.2. FNR, Precision, and Selection Rate for Model Recommendations for O-5 Promotions, by Gender and Cutoff

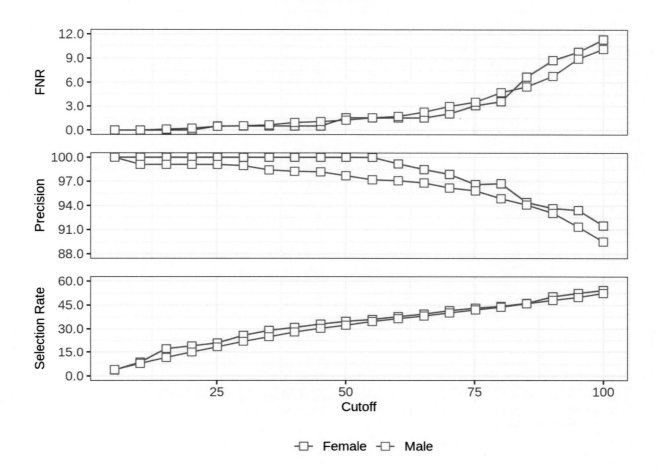

We then computed fairness separately for each board. Table A.2 shows the selection rates, FNR, and precision for male and female officers, by board. As in Table A.1, these metrics are worse for both groups in 2019, although they did not tend to selectively disadvantage male or female officers during any year.

Table A.2. Selection Rate, FNR, and Precision for Model Recommendations for O-6 Promotions, by Gender and Year

O-6 Board	Cutoff	Selection Rate		FNR		Precision	
		Female (%)	Male (%)	Female (%)	Male (%)	Female (%)	Male (%)
2012	10	15.0	10.0	0.0	0.0	100	100
2014	10	0.0	0.0	0.0	0.0	NA[a]	NA[a]
2015	10	0.0	11.0	0.0	0.0	NA[a]	86.4
2016	10	11.1	10.4	0.0	0.0	100	100
2019	10	0.0	0.0	0.0	5.1	NA[a]	NA[a]
2012	25	25.0	16.9	0.0	0.0	100	92.3
2014	25	0.0	0.0	0.0	0.0	NA[a]	NA[a]
2015	25	0.0	14.0	0.0	0.0	NA[a]	89.3
2016	25	16.7	20.0	0.0	0.0	100	96.3
2019	25	6.7	4.3	11.1	10.1	0.0	83.3
2012	50	25.0	21.2	0.0	2.3	100	89.8
2014	50	5.3	9.7	0.0	4.4	100	95.0
2015	50	5.9	23.0	0.0	1.2	100	89.1
2016	50	27.8	27.4	0.0	1.4	100	91.9
2019	50	20.0	24.1	22.2	10.1	66.7	88.2

[a] A precision value of NA implies that no candidates received the "Select" recommendation because none was clearly distinguishable from the gray zone. All candidates who received automated recommendations in this scenario received "Do not select."

Appendix B. Testing Fairness in Recommendation Cutoffs

To generate promotion recommendations, the ML system described in Chapter 5 uses a trained model to (1) predict the promotion probability for each officer, (2) sort officers based on these probabilities, (3) identify the final officer selected to meet the promotion quota, and (4) find a percentage of officers furthest from this "pivot" candidate. The ML system recommends "Select" for officers who are highest in the upper tail of the promotion probability distribution and "Do not select" for the ones in the lower tail. For example, given a cutoff of 10 percent, the ML system will identify and issue recommendations for the 10 percent of officers with predicted probabilities furthest from the pivot candidate.

Using gender as the protected characteristic, we evaluated fairness for different values of the cutoff (Figure B.1). If selection rates between groups (i.e., male and female officers) violate the 80/20 rule, this indicates that ML recommendations, given that value of the cutoff, are not fair.

Figure B.1. Distribution of O-6 Promotion Odds (Top) and Ratio of Female to Male Selections for Different Cutoffs (Bottom)

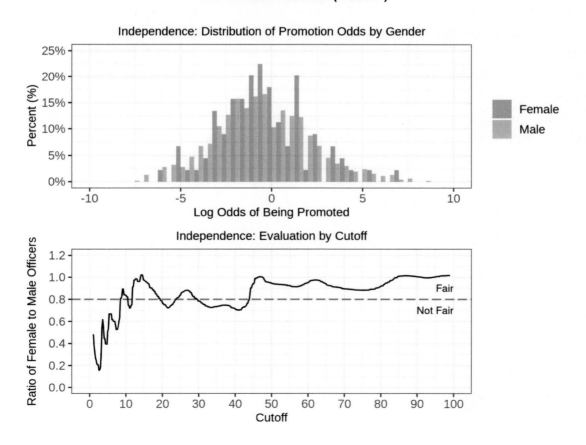

To evaluate whether certain cutoffs satisfy independence, consider the distribution of promotion odds in the top panel of Figure B.1. We label the distribution $f_A(x)$, where A is 0 if an individual is male and 1 if an individual is female. For a given threshold, τ, selection rate for a group is the solution to the integral,

$$\int_\tau^\infty f_A(x)\,dx.$$

To approximate the integral, we fit 1-dimensional splines to the distributions in Figure B.1 and applied off-the-shelf numerical integration methods. To generate selection rates for all possible thresholds, we repeated the numerical integration for different values of τ.

For each value of τ, we computed the ratio of selection rates between female and male officers,

$$\frac{\int_\tau^\infty f_{A=1}(x)\,dx}{\int_\tau^\infty f_{A=0}(x)\,dx}.$$

The selection ratios are shown in the bottom panel of Figure B.1 as a function of cutoff. Values above the red line denote violations of the 80/20 rule. As can be seen, thresholds below 10 percent, from 18 to 22 percent, and from 28 to 40 percent violate the 80/20 rule. The DAF could use this type of analysis to select thresholds to reduce rater workload without violating the fairness criterion.

Separation can also be found without loss of generality. To do this, we repeated the previous analysis for the subset of individuals who were selected for promotion. Figure B.2 shows the results.

Figure B.2. Distribution of O-6 Promotion Odds (Top) and Ratio of Female to Male Selections for Different Cutoffs (Bottom) for Officers Selected for Promotion

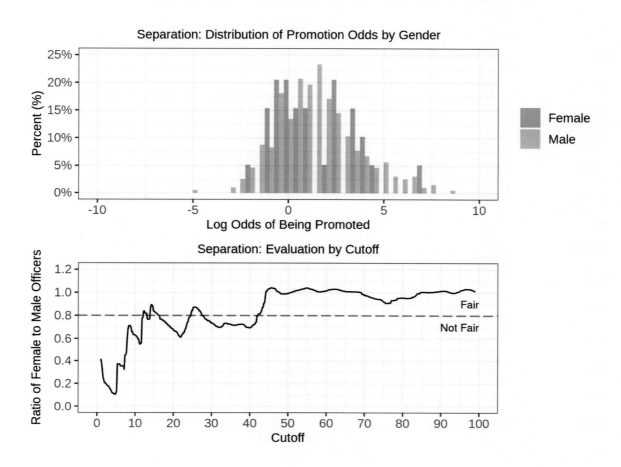

Abbreviations

AI	artificial intelligence
DAF	Department of the Air Force
DE	developmental education
DoD	U.S. Department of Defense
DT&E	development test and evaluation
FNR	false negative rate
HR	human resources
HRM	human resource management
IDE	Intermediate Development Education
MAE	mean absolute error
ML	machine learning
MoE	measures of effectiveness
MoP	measures of performance
MSE	mean squared error
NLP	natural language processing
OPR	officer performance report
OSR	officer selection records
OT&E	operational test and evaluation
PRF	promotion recommendation form
SA	situational awareness
SDE	Senior Development Education
USAF	U.S. Air Force

References

Arrieta, Alejandro Barredo, Natalia Díaz-Rodríguez, Javier Del Ser, Adrien Bennetot, Siham Tabik, Alberto Barbado, Salvador García, Sergio Gil-López, Daniel Molina, Richard Benjamins, et al., "Explainable Artificial Intelligence (XAI): Concepts, Taxonomies, Opportunities and Challenges Toward Responsible AI," *Information Fusion*, Vol. 58, 2020.

Barocas, Solon, Moritz Hardt, and Arvind Narayanan, *Fairness and Machine Learning: Limitations and Opportunities*, MIT Press, 2023.

Brown, Charles Q., *CSAF Action Orders to Accelerate Change Across Air Force*, Chief of Staff, U.S. Air Force, December 2020.

Cabreros, Irineo, Joshua Snoke, Osonde A. Osoba, Inez Khan, and Marc N. Elliott, *Advancing Equitable Decisionmaking for the Department of Defense Through Fairness in Machine Learning*, RAND Corporation, RR-A1542-1, 2023. As of December 29, 2023:
https://www.rand.org/pubs/research_reports/RRA1542-1.html

Calkins, Avery, Monique Graham, Claude Messan Setodji, David Schulker, and Matthew Walsh, *Machine Learning–Enabled Recommendations for the Air Force Officer Assignment System:* Vol. 5, RAND Corporation, RR-A1745-5, 2024.

Caruana, Rich, Yin Lou, Johannes Gehrke, Paul Koch, Marc Sturm, and Noemie Elhadad, "Intelligible Models for Healthcare: Predicting Pneumonia Risk and Hospital 30-Day Readmission," in *Proceedings of the 21st ACM SIGKDD International Conference on Knowledge Discovery and Data Mining*, Sydney, Australia, Association for Computing Machinery, 2015.

Center for Security and Emerging Technology, homepage, 2021. As of December 29, 2023:
https://cset.georgetown.edu/

Chui, Michael, Bryce Hall, Alex Singla, and Alex Sukharevsky, "The State of AI in 2021," McKinsey & Company, December 8, 2021. As of December 29, 2023:
https://www.mckinsey.com/business-functions/quantumblack/our-insights/global-survey-the-state-of-ai-in-2021

Code of Federal Regulations, Title 29, Subtitle B, Chapter 14, Part 1607.4 (D) (eCFR :: 29 CFR Part 1607—Uniform Guidelines on Employee Selection Procedures (1978).

Corbett-Davies, Sam, Emma Pierson, Avi Feller, Sharad Goel, and Aziz Huq, "Algorithmic Decision Making and the Cost of Fairness," paper presented at *Proceedings of the 23rd ACM SIGKDD International Conference on Knowledge Discovery and Data Mining*, Halifax, NS, Canada, Association for Computing Machinery, 2017.

DAF—*See* U.S. Department of the Air Force.

DoD—*See* U.S. Department of Defense.

Doshi-Velez, Finale, and Been Kim, "Towards a Rigorous Science of Interpretable Machine Learning," ArXiv preprint 1702.08608, 2017. As of December 29, 2023: https://arxiv.org/abs/1702.08608

Fjeld, Jessica, Nele Achten, Hannah Hilligoss, Adam Nagy, and Madhulika Srikumar, "Principled Artificial Intelligence: Mapping Consensus in Ethical and Rights-Based Approaches to Principles for AI," Berkman Klein Center Research Publication No. 2020-1, February 14, 2021. As of December 29, 2023: https://papers.ssrn.com/sol3/papers.cfm?abstract_id=3518482

Fox, Maria, Derek Long, and Daniele Magazzeni, "Explainable Planning," 2017. As of December 29, 2023: https://arxiv.org/abs/1709.10256

Guenole, Nigel, and Sheri Feinzig, *The Business Case for AI in HR: Insights and Tips on Getting Started*, IBM, November 2018. As of December 29, 2023: https://www.ibm.com/downloads/cas/A5YLEPBR

Hoffman, Robert R., Shane T. Mueller, Gary Klein, and Jordan Litman, "Metrics for Explainable AI: Challenges and Prospects," 2018. As of December 29, 2023: https://arxiv.org/abs/1812.04608

Joint Artificial Intelligence Center, "AI Ethical Principles—Highlighting the Progress and Future of Responsible AI in the DoD," *Intelligence Office Blog*, Chief Digital and Artificial Intelligence Office, February 26, 2021. As of December 29, 2023: https://www.ai.mil/blog_02_26_21-ai_ethics_principles-highlighting_the_progress_and_future_of_responsible_ai.html

Jordan, Michael I., and Tom M. Mitchell, "Machine Learning: Trends, Perspectives, and Prospects," *Science*, Vol. 349, No. 6245, July 17, 2015. As of December 29, 2023: https://www.science.org/lookup/doi/10.1126/science.aaa8415

Kleinberg, Jon, Sendhil Mullainathan, and Manish Raghavan, "Inherent Trade-Offs in the Fair Determination of Risk Scores," 2016. As of December 29, 2023: https://arxiv.org/abs/1609.05807

Kordzadeh, Nima, and Maryam Ghasemaghaei, "Algorithmic Bias: Review, Synthesis, and Future Research Directions," *European Journal of Information Systems*, Vol. 31, No. 3, 2022.

Lipton, Zachary C., "The Mythos of Model Interpretability," paper presented at 2016 ICML Workshop on Human Interpretability in Machine Learning (WHI 2016), New York, 2017.

Mohseni, Sina, Niloofar Zarei, and Eric D. Ragan, "A Multidisciplinary Survey and Framework for Design and Evaluation of Explainable AI Systems," *ACM Transactions on Interactive Intelligent Systems (TiiS)*, Vol. 11, No. 3–4, 2021.

Myatt, Summer, "Air Force's Data Fabric in Maturation Stage, Officials Say," *GovConWire*, March 30, 2022. As of January 2, 2024:
https://www.govconwire.com/2022/03/air-forces-data-fabric-in-maturation-stage-officials-say/

National Security Commission on Artificial Intelligence, *Final Report*, undated. As of December 29, 2023:
https://reports.nscai.gov/final-report/table-of-contents/

Neural Information Processing Systems, NeurIPS 2021, virtual conference, December 6–14, 2021. As of January 19, 2024:
https://neurips.cc/Conferences/2021

Parasuraman, Raja, and Victor Riley, "Humans and Automation: Use, Misuse, Disuse, Abuse," *Human Factors*, Vol. 39, No. 2, 1997.

Parasuraman, Raja, Thomas B. Sheridan, and Christopher D. Wickens, "A Model for Types and Levels of Human Interaction with Automation," *IEEE Transactions on Systems, Man, and Cybernetics–Part A: Systems and Humans*, Vol. 30, No. 3: 2000.

Rudin, Cynthia, "Stop Explaining Black Box Machine Learning Models for High Stakes Decisions and Use Interpretable Models Instead," *Nature Machine Intelligence*, Vol. 1, No. 5, 2019.

Russel, Stuart, and Peter Norvig, *Introduction to Artificial Intelligence: A Modern Approach*, Prentice-Hall of India, 1995.

Schulker, David, Joshua Williams, Cheryl K. Montemayor, Li Ang Zhang, and Matthew Walsh, *The Personnel Records Scoring System*: Vol. 3, *A Methodology for Designing Tools to Support Air Force Human Resources Decisionmaking*, RAND Corporation, RR-A1745-3, 2024.

Schulker, David, Matthew Walsh, Avery Calkins, Monique Graham, Cheryl K. Montemayor, Albert A. Robbert, Sean Robson, Claude Messan Setodji, Joshua Snoke, Joshua Williams, and Li Ang Zhang, *Leveraging Machine Learning to Improve Human Resource Management:* Vol. 1, *Key Findings and Recommendations for Policymakers*, RAND Corporation, RR-A1745-1, 2024.

Schulker, David, Joshua Williams, Cheryl K. Montemayor, Li Ang Zhang, and Matthew Walsh, *The Personnel Records Scoring System:* Vol. 3, *A Methodology for Designing Tools to Support Air Force Human Resources Decisionmaking*, RAND Corporation, RR-A1745-3, 2024.

Secretary of Defense, "Actions to Improve Racial and Ethnic Diversity and Inclusion in the U.S. Military," memorandum, Department of Defense, December 17, 2020.

Steinberg, Daniel, Alistair Reid, and Simon O'Callaghan, "Fairness Measures for Regression via Probabilistic Classification," 2020. As of December 29, 2023:
https://arxiv.org/abs/2001.06089

USAF—*See* U.S. Air Force.

U.S. Air Force, *Artificial Intelligence Annex to the Department of Defense Artificial Intelligence Strategy*, 2019.

U.S. Department of Defense, *Summary of the 2018 Department of Defense Artificial Intelligence Strategy: Harnessing AI to Advance Our Security and Prosperity*, 2018.

U.S. Department of Defense, *Responsible Artificial Intelligence Strategy and Implementation Pathway*, 2022.

U.S. Department of the Air Force, Air Force Instruction 36-2301, *Developmental Education*, July 16, 2010.

U.S. Department of the Air Force, Air Force Instruction 1-1, *Air Force Culture: Air Force Standards*, August 7, 2012, incorporating Change 1, November 12, 2014.

U.S. Department of the Air Force, Air Force Instruction 36-7001, *Diversity and Inclusion, Department of the Air Force*, 2019a.

U.S. Department of the Air Force, Air Force Instruction 36-2406, *Officer and Enlisted Evaluations Systems*, Department of the Air Force, November 14, 2019b.

U.S. Department of the Air Force, Air Force Instruction 36-2501, *Officer Promotion and Selective Continuation,* April 30, 2021.

Walsh, Matthew, Lance Menthe, Edward Geist, Eric Hastings, Joshua Kerrigan, Jasmin Léveillé, Joshua Margolis, Nicholas Martin, and Brian P. Donnelly, *Exploring the Feasibility and Utility of Machine Learning–Assisted Command and Control:* Vol. 1, *Findings and Recommendations*, RAND Corporation, RR-A263-1, 2021. As of December 29, 2023:
https://www.rand.org/pubs/research_reports/RRA263-1.html

Walsh, Matthew, Sean Robson, Albert A. Robbert, and David Schulker, *Machine Learning in Air Force Human Resource Management:* Vol. 2, *A Framework for Vetting Use Cases with Example Applications*, RAND Corporation, RR-A1745-2, 2024.

Zhang, Daniel, Nestor Maslej, Erik Brynjolfsson, John Etchemendy, Terah Lyons, James Manyika, Helen Ngo, Juan Carlos Niebles, Michael Sellitto, Ellie Sakhaee, et al., *The AI Index 2022 Annual Report*, AI Index Steering Committee, Stanford Institute for Human-Centered AI, Stanford University, March 2022. As of December 29, 2023: https://aiindex.stanford.edu/ai-index-report-2022/